English Your Questions Answered

Michael McCarthy

Prolinguam Publishing

Copyright © Michael McCarthy 2017
All rights reserved

Please respect this copyright. No part of this publication may be reproduced, stored in a retrieval system or transmitted in any form or by any means without the prior written permission of the copyright holder, except for short quotations for the purposes of review.

First published 2017 by
Prolinguam Publishing
CB23 2RW
UK

Minor changes have been made to the wording of this edition compared with that of the e-book edition of 2017 for formatting reasons

Cover illustration by tebbitdesign, tebbitdesign.co.uk

Dedicated to the memory of Amorey Gethin,
mentor, friend and fellow-traveller

ACKNOWLEDGEMENTS

Many thanks to the following, without whom this book would never have seen the light of day: academic colleagues and associates at the universities of Birmingham, Nottingham, Limerick, Cornell, Penn State, Valencia, Newcastle and Cambridge for years of shared ideas and insights; my late friend, Amorey Gethin, the first and most important mentor of my teaching career; Mr Brian Mark, my secondary school English teacher; his daughter, applied linguist and grammarian Geraldine Mark, for her review and professional editing of the manuscript; Professor Michael Handford, internationally renowned corpus linguist, for his review of the manuscript; Professor Ronald Carter, friend, colleague, co-author and professional partner of more than 30 years; the late Dr David Brazil, mentor, colleague, friend, a most original thinker in the fields of grammar and phonetics; Dr Anne O'Keeffe, co-author and corpus researcher in grammar and pragmatics; Dr Felicity O'Dell for years of co-authoring books on English vocabulary; Michael Swan, professional friend and extraordinarily perceptive grammarian; the late Professor John Sinclair, pioneer of corpus linguistics, who taught me everything about using and interpreting language corpora; Alban Fernandez for his excellent and careful proofreading and formatting of the manuscript; Jake Tebbit, graphic artist and illustrator, for his talent as reflected in the cover design of this book; and finally, thanks to my wife, co-author and co-researcher, Jeanne McCarten, for the best and happiest days of my life.

ABOUT THE AUTHOR

Michael McCarthy was born and grew up in Cardiff. He studied at Downing College, Cambridge from 1966 to 1973, where he received his MA and PhD. He later trained to be an English teacher at the University of Leeds.
He is Emeritus Professor of Applied Linguistics in the School of English, University of Nottingham, UK. He has also served as Visiting Professor in Applied Linguistics at the University of Limerick, Ireland, and Newcastle University, UK, and as Adjunct Professor at Penn State University, USA. He holds an Honorary Professorship at the University of Valencia, Spain. For the last 30 years, he has worked with large, computerised corpora of English texts, investigating them to establish how the vocabulary and grammar of English are used at the present time and how they are evolving and changing.
He is author/co-author of more than 50 books and over 100 academic papers dealing with the description and teaching of the English language, especially as a second or foreign language and with a focus on the spoken language. He has taught in Britain, The Netherlands, Spain, Sweden and Malaysia. He is co-author of the 900-page *Cambridge Grammar of English*, *Grammar for Business*, *English Grammar Today* and the globally successful *Touchstone* and *Viewpoint* courses for adult learners of English (all published by Cambridge University Press).
He has lectured in 46 countries on aspects of English and English teaching and has spoken about grammar in radio and TV interviews in different parts of the world.

Contents

WHO IS THIS BOOK FOR?	1
FINDING THE EVIDENCE FOR 'GOOD GRAMMAR'	2
A THINKING PERSON'S GUIDE	3
WHAT IS GRAMMAR?	4
SPEAKING and WRITING	5
DIALECTS and STANDARD ENGLISH	6
HOW TO USE THIS BOOK	7
TERMINOLOGY	7
WHAT ELSE?	8
GRAMMAR A-Z	9
ACCOMMODATION	9
ADVERBS (WELL, SUDDENLY)	9
AFFECT or EFFECT	9
AGREEMENT (CONCORD)	10
ALL and ALL OF	15
ALL RIGHT or ALRIGHT	16
ALL TOGETHER or ALTOGETHER	16
ALTERNATE or ALTERNATIVE	16
A LOT and ALOT	16
AMERICAN INFLUENCES	17
AMOUNT OF or NUMBER OF	20
ANACOLUTHIA	21
ANOTHER	21
ANY MORE or ANYMORE	22
APOSTROPHES	22
AROUND and ROUND	26
AS and LIKE	27
AS LONG AS and SO LONG AS	28
BESIDE or BESIDES	28
BETWEEN or AMONG	28
BETWEEN YOU AND ME	29
-CE or -SE: (PRACTICE, PRACTISE)	29
CAN, MAY and MIGHT	30
CAPITAL LETTERS	30

CLICHÉS	32
COLON	33
COMMA	33
COMPARE TO and COMPARE WITH	38
COMPARATIVES (BIGGER, EASIER)	39
CONTINUOUS and CONTINUAL	40
CONTRACTIONS	41
CONTRIBUTE, DISTRIBUTE (PRONUNCIATION)	42
COUNTRIES	42
CREATIVE WORD-FORMATION	43
CRITERION/CRITERIA, PHENOMENON/PHENOMENA	45
DASHES	46
DATA	46
DEFINITE(LY)	47
DIFFERENT TO, FROM, THAN	47
DOUBLE IS (THE THING IS IS …)	48
DOUBLE NEGATIVES	48
DUE TO and OWING TO	49
DUNNO, GONNA, GOTTA, WANNA	50
EACH OTHER and ONE ANOTHER	50
EITHER and NEITHER	51
ELLIPSIS (POSTMAN BEEN YET?)	51
ENDINGS IN -WARD or -WARDS (TOWARD[S])	52
ESPECIALLY and SPECIALLY	53
EVERY DAY and EVERYDAY	53
EXCLAMATION MARK	54
FARTHER/-EST or FURTHER/-EST	54
FIRST(LY), SECOND(LY)	55
FULL STOP	56
GAOL and JAIL	56
GET	57
GO IN SPEECH REPORTS (HE GOES, "WHERE ARE YOU?")	58
H- IN WORDS LIKE HISTORIC AND HOTEL	59
HAD BETTER	59
HARDLY and HARD	59

HAS YET TO and IS YET TO	60
HEADERS and TAILS (MY SON, JAMES, HE'S A PILOT)	60
HE/SHE, HE OR SHE, THEY (EVERY CITIZEN SHOULD DO THEIR DUTY)	61
HYPHENS	62
IF: THINGS TO LOOK OUT FOR	64
IT'S or ITS	65
KIND, SORT and TYPE	65
LESS and FEWER	66
LET'S	67
LIE or LAY	67
LIKE (IT WAS CRAZY, LIKE!)	68
LIKELY	69
LOAN WORDS (KEBAB, MACHO)	69
MADE OF, FROM, WITH, OUT OF	70
MALAPROPISMS (ACRIMONIAL DEBATES)	71
MAY BE and MAYBE	72
MEDIA	72
METER and METRE	72
MISPLACED PARTICIPLES (A HARE DRIVING HOME)	73
MISS	73
MISS, MS, MRS, MR, MASTER	73
NEVERTHELESS and NONETHELESS	74
NOUNS, VERBS, ADJECTIVES: TYPES OF WORDS	74
OFF	75
OLDER, ELDER, OLDEST and ELDEST	76
ONES and ONE'S	76
PAST and PASSED	77
PAST TENSE (TOOK) and PAST PARTICIPLE (TAKEN)	77
PHRASES, CLAUSES, SENTENCES	79
PREFIXES (UN-, IN-, DIS-)	80
PREPOSITIONS (TO, FROM, OF)	82
PRINCIPAL and PRINCIPLE	83
PRONOUNS (I, ME, WE, US, THEY, THEM)	84
PRONOUNS ENDING IN -ONE AND -BODY (ANYONE, SOMEBODY)	85
PROVIDED and PROVIDING (THAT)	86

QUESTION MARK	86
QUOTATION MARKS / INVERTED COMMAS ("...")	88
RAISE, RISE and ARISE	89
REFLEXIVE PRONOUNS (MYSELF, YOURSELF)	90
REGARD (WITH REGARD TO, AS REGARDS)	92
RELATIVE CLAUSES (THE GIRL WHO WON THE PRIZE)	92
RIGHT(LY), WRONG(LY)	93
SEMICOLON	94
SHALL and WILL	95
SIGHT or SITE	95
SINGULAR USE OF THEY/THEM/THEIR	96
SO	96
SOME TIME or SOMETIME	97
SPLIT INFINITIVES	97
SUBJECTS and OBJECTS	97
SUBJUNCTIVE (I INSIST THAT HE APOLOGISE)	98
SUFFIXES (-FUL, -ITY)	99
SUPERLATIVE (BEST, MOST FRIGHTENING)	104
TAUTOLOGY (A ROUND SPHERE)	104
THE and TO: PRONUNCIATION	105
THERE IS and THERE ARE	106
THERE, THERE'S, THEIR and THEIRS	106
THOSE and THEM	107
TILL and UNTIL	107
TOO or TO	107
TURNED (A)ROUND AND ...	108
VAGUE EXPRESSIONS (THINGS LIKE THAT)	108
WHILE and WHILST	109
WHO, WHOM, WHOSE, WHICH, THAT and WHAT	109
YOU'RE and YOUR	111
Z: THE LETTER	111
ZEUGMA	111
BACKGROUND READING AND RESOURCES	113

WHO IS THIS BOOK FOR?

The book is primarily designed for people whose native or first language is the English of Britain and Ireland but who have occasional doubts about what is considered correct and what is not correct in grammar. It's not specifically designed for language learners, but if you're an expert non-native user of English, you might find it useful. If you speak another variety of English (e.g. American, Nigerian, Australian, Indian) you should find that most, but not all, of the grammar in this book corresponds with the standard conventions of your variety.

This is not a complete reference grammar of English. Nor is it one of those well-intentioned manuals that bog you down in differences between gerunds and gerundives. It focuses instead on the problems that native and expert non-native users of English often encounter concerning the best choice of grammar to suit their purpose. The book is aimed at sorting out perennial problems and chasing off phantoms that lurk in the background while we're trying to speak or write 'properly'. All 'properly' means here is 'according to the agreed, standard conventions of the time'.

Shakespeare famously used a number of what we now call double comparatives and double superlatives such as *more hotter, more worse* and *most bravest.* These have fallen out of usage and are now considered 'bad grammar'. So, remember, 'good grammar' changes over time and all this book is trying to do is to help you to feel comfortable with what is widely accepted as standard usage in this decade. Things are not always 100% clear-cut, so be prepared to go away with decisions to make and something to think about, rather than always being dished up truths and certainties, which are most likely to turn out to be untruths and uncertainties or, if they aren't already, might well be so in a couple of years from now.

FINDING THE EVIDENCE FOR 'GOOD GRAMMAR'

Grammarians are specialists who try to observe and describe how we all speak and write. One type of grammarian does this by sitting down with a cup of tea or a stiff drink while pondering inwardly on what they feel to be correct or incorrect. In the old days, most of them were male academics or gentleman scholars, and they would lock their office doors and light up a pipe to help them concentrate.

Some grammarians get their grammar from past grammars that have been published and then just update them. Sometimes they add a dose of introspection, bits of grammar they were taught in school and brainwaves they get amid the pipe-smoke.

All of the above methods can result in odd, dotty or even downright erroneous versions of grammar.

A more reliable method is to observe how people use grammar and to make field notes. You do this by reading books, newspapers, letters, websites, blogs, emails, etc., listening to radio and TV and shamelessly eavesdropping on people's conversations in public spaces. If you gather enough field notes on a particular point of grammar, you can start to craft a statement about current usage. Field notes have a long and respectable history in the study of language.

More recently, grammarians have interrogated big computer databases of 'used' language (books, newspapers, websites, broadcasts, transcribed conversations) called *corpora* (the plural of *corpus*, meaning a body of texts) by applying dedicated software to the data to let the computer ascertain how language is really used. The software can reveal what the most (and least) frequently used words and patterns of grammar are and can show the typical contexts in which grammatical forms occur. By analysing hundreds of thousands of real examples, grammarians can produce more reliable and realistic versions of grammar.

What's more, computers have no prejudices and never went to school, so what they tell us is dispassionate and about as objective as you're likely to get.

I've worked with corpora for 30 years and what you'll find in this book is based on my field notes, which I check by looking at different British and American English corpora, a number of which are available for consultation online. I look to see if my field notes are just observations of oddities and idiosyncrasies or whether they are evidence of widespread use, as evidenced in corpora. I then try to distil my years of observations and corpus research into straightforward guidelines and clear examples that I hope you will find to be both informative and enjoyable, and which illustrate how people actually use the language, as opposed to how we think they do or ought to do.

A THINKING PERSON'S GUIDE

Intelligent, thinking people don't just follow rules or social conventions blindly. They like to know a bit about how they work, reflect on them and, if necessary, challenge them or simply ignore them. So, you won't be fined or go to prison if you break the conventions of grammar as laid out in this book. They are there for you to exploit them to the best ends, whether to feel satisfied that you're using the most widely accepted conventions, to create a desired impression or to be purposely creative with grammar.

Sometimes I'll be strict and conventional and say that something is standard or non-standard when the evidence clearly comes down heavily and unambiguously on one side or another. But the scales don't always fall decisively in one direction or another. Therefore, sometimes I'll invite you to make your own choice, or say it doesn't really matter because two or more acceptable ways of saying something are in widespread and common use. Often, the choices you have to make will depend on the situation, whether formal or informal, written or spoken.

Here and there I mention what grammarians of former centuries have said. This is not to impress you that I am a brainy professor. It is simply to show how things change, how some aspects of grammar have been debated for centuries, and how the rules of grammar handed down through the generations have their origins in classically-dominated scholarship and in particular social and political environments.

Academics are notorious for fudging and hedging, but I'll try to keep that to a minimum. In the end, you must decide what to say or write. You're a thinking person.

WHAT IS GRAMMAR?

Think of grammar as a set of conventions that evolve over time. As in any kind of natural selection, the most viable forms adapt and survive, new forms evolve and some forms become as dead as the dodo. Grammar changes to adapt itself to the environment in which it operates, just like Darwin's finches.

Don't think of grammar as a set of rules like legal statutes or the rules of chess. There are no grammar police (well, apart from teachers, examiners, the occasional pompous politician or journalist, and letters-to-the-editor writers with too much time on their hands). Grammar didn't come down from the skies and nobody came across it carved on tablets of stone. Grammar is a set of collective agreements about how we communicate. And the collective agreements change over time.

As with all social conventions, people judge one another on whether they adhere to them. Show up to a beach party in a formal business suit and people may think you're odd. Go for an interview for a job in a city bank dressed in a swimming costume, flippers and snorkel, and you probably won't get the job. Be careless with your grammar in your cv or professional correspondence and you'll probably be judged in some way not favourable to you.

Grammar isn't all that difficult or mysterious, but it can seem a bit fiddly. Basically, there are two parts to it. First there are the components. The main components are words. Words fall into different types (nouns, verbs, pronouns, prepositions, etc.). And then there are components like apostrophe *'s*, plural *-(e)s*, past tense *-ed* and present participle *-ing*, and symbols such as commas, full stops and question marks.

Next there's how we order the components. We say *I have never been there before*, not *I been have never before there*. The ordering of the components is sometimes called *syntax*. Impress your friends with that one.

SPEAKING and WRITING

The 18th century grammarian, James Greenwood, in his *Royal English Grammar* of 1737, had his eye on the different knowledge required for speech and for writing:

For tho' it is possible that a Young Gentleman or Lady may be enabled to speak well upon some Subjects, and entertain a Visitor with Discourse agreeable enough; yet I do not well see how they should write any Thing with a tolerable Correctness unless they have some Taste of Grammar, or express themselves clearly, or deliver their Thoughts by Letter or otherwise, so as not to lay themselves open to the Censure of their Friends ...

Throughout this book you will come across references to things that are acceptable in everyday conversation but less so in contexts such as formal correspondence or situations such as formal meetings or job interviews. The grammar of speaking and the grammar of writing draw on the same resources but in different ways.

Everyday conversation happens in real time; it is created online, so to speak. All sorts of things that purists frown upon in writing go unnoticed in everyday speech and are often used by the very same purists themselves.

Any politician, journalist or Prince of the Blood Royal who rails against 'sloppy' usage such as *gonna* and *dunno* instead of *going to* and *don't know* should listen in to a live debate in Parliament, where these forms are commonly heard – though they're usually 'tidied up' for the official record, as Rebecca Hughes's excellent 1996 book *English in Speech and Writing* demonstrates.

The most important thing is to be aware of the different demands grammar places on us in different situations. If you grew up speaking one of the many lovely regional dialects of English and then had it drained out of you through years of education, you may yet feel most comfortable slipping back into your dialect grammar and vocabulary when you go back to your original community or meet up with old friends. That's a far cry from writing a formal business letter or email, or being on the receiving end of a crucial job interview, where you want to identify with a different community. It's horses for courses.

DIALECTS and STANDARD ENGLISH

Dialects are simply different ways of speaking and writing within the same language. Dialects are often seen as inferior or something to be shed as you climb the socio-economic greasy pole, because dialects differ from the most widely accepted educated standard. Dialects are not inferior to any other way of using language. It just so happens that, because they are often rooted in geographical regions or social groups, they are considered different and non-standard when compared with whatever dialect has achieved the powerful status of nation-wide use in education, literature and the media. Whenever I mention 'standard' or 'standard forms' in this book, I am talking about majority usage across a wide range of educated speakers and writers in the United Kingdom and Ireland, based on my years of researching different corpora (computer databases) of written and spoken English, my fieldwork and observation of usage in the media and in the English of people going about their everyday business. Occasionally I also have recourse to commonly accepted standards derived from trustworthy reference grammars. I make no negative value judgements of dialect forms, but I do bring to your attention those that are sometimes infelicitously mixed with educated-standard forms. I advise that non-standard forms should be used as and when appropriate and that you become aware of them in your own usage, whether you are a speaker of a 'posh' or 'toff's' dialect or a regional, rural or urban dialect, or one associated with a particular social class or community. The important thing is to know what is and what is not suitable in any given situation and to choose appropriately.

HOW TO USE THIS BOOK

You can just read it from cover to cover if you wish and if you've got the time. I would be most flattered. There's a table of contents at the beginning of the book and the whole book is organised A-Z with cross-references, so you have various ways into it.

TERMINOLOGY

In this book, you'll come across terminology you may be unfamiliar with or which you only vaguely remember from school. There is a vast amount of grammatical terminology that linguists use, but most of it is unnecessary to our current purpose, so I hope you will not drown in jargon and give up the struggle. The most important terms (e.g. subjects and objects, prepositions, reflexive pronouns, superlatives) have their own headings. Other terms will be introduced and explained as we go along, but only if necessary.

WHAT ELSE?

Some words are notoriously difficult to spell. English spelling got stuck somewhere along the line historically and we're left with some frustrating problems like sequences of vowels, spelling of plurals, double consonants and so on. Because of this, I've included some words that people often spell incorrectly. There are also some cases where pronunciation varies. Everything else we can cover as we go along. I hope you enjoy the book.

GRAMMAR A-Z

ACCOMMODATION
Note the spelling: *-cc- -mm-*. Traditionally, British English treats this as a mass (uncountable) noun, so it is not used in the plural.
They have some wonderful **accommodation** for students on campus these days, not like when I was at university.
However, American English has long been happy with plural *accommodations* in sentences like the above and you'll occasionally see and hear it in British English too.

ADVERBS (WELL, SUDDENLY)
Convention has it that most adverbs end in *-ly*, though some everyday adverbs don't (*well, fast, better, worse, hard* [as in *work hard*], *inside*, etc.). The following are non-standard:
It all happened very **sudden**. (= *suddenly*)
She did really **good** in her exams. (= *well*)
Norman Blake's 2004 book, *Shakespeare's Non-Standard English*, has a long list of adjectives used as adverbs (e.g. *thou didst it excellent* [modern usage: *excellently*], from *Taming of the Shrew*).
I grew up in South Wales, where adverbs without *-ly* were considered as normal as being able to sing in harmony. Our national poet, Dylan Thomas, famously referred to the boys *dreaming wicked* in his immortal *Under Milk Wood*.
See HARDLY AND HARD, RIGHT(LY), WRONG(LY), TIGHT(LY).

AFFECT or EFFECT
This is one you may keep coming back to.
Affect is a verb meaning to influence someone or something.
*Solar flares can **affect** radio communications on earth.*
*We were deeply **affected** by the sad news.*
The complications come with *effect*. As a noun, its meaning is

9

related to the verb *affect* and it means 'influence or result'.
*The **effects** of the storm were felt over a large area.*
*Did that cough medicine you bought have any **effect**?*
It's also used in the phrase *special effects*.
*That movie had some amazing **special effects**.*
Effect can also be used as a verb meaning 'to achieve' or 'bring about', but it's rather formal and you can happily live without it.
*The National Executive has **effected** some basic changes in the party structure.*

AGREEMENT (CONCORD)
Subject-verb concord (I work, she works)
This is mostly about making sure the subject and verb don't clash in terms of number.

Except for the verb *to be*, English verbs are straightforward in the present tense, unlike heavily-inflected languages, where verbs can have lots of complicated endings. All you need to do is to add *-s* (or *-es*) when you refer to a third person singular entity (i.e. not *I, you* or *we*).

***He** work**s** for a software company and **his wife** runs a big charity organisation.*
***My dad** watch**es** all kinds of sport on TV but **he** never do**es** any himself.*

When the subject is a plural noun or pronoun, no *-s* is used:
***My friends** all **live** miles away.*

Nouns that are always plural (politics, economics)
Some nouns are always plural, for example the names of many academic disciplines (*economics, politics, physics*). These are used with a singular verb:

*Quantum mechanics **is** beyond me. I think you need a brain the size of a planet to understand it all.*
*Politics **is** a popular subject at universities these days.*

However, when *politics* refers to a person's ideology or attitudes, it is general used with a plural verb:

*Her politics **are** quite right wing. I was surprised.*

Ben Jonson, in his *The English Grammar* of 1640, *Made by Ben Jonson for the benefit of all Strangers out of his observation of the English Language now spoken and in use*, tackles the issue of agreement with always-plural nouns, reminding us that there's not much new under the sun:

*In this exception of number, the verb sometime agreeth not with the governing noun of the plural number, as it should, but with the noun governed: as Riches **is** a thing oft-times more hurtful than profitable to the owners.*

*Riches **are** a thing most people can only dream of* would do just as well nowadays.

Subjects linked by *and* (Geoff and his brother were there)

When subjects are linked by *and*, be careful not to be fooled by a singular noun before the verb:

<u>Geoff and his brother</u> ***was*** there. (non-standard)

<u>Geoff and his brother</u> ***were*** there. (standard)

Just recently, an expert interviewed on the BBC, commenting on dubious health claims made by certain food products, said:

*Nutritional and health claims **is** very important.*

The verb should be plural (<u>*are*</u> *very important*) but the speaker was probably thinking of nutritional and health claims taken together as one important issue, so psychologically just a single idea. This kind of psychological concord is more common than one might expect, and you may want to keep an eye out for it in your own speaking and writing so that you don't do it in inappropriate contexts (i.e. more formal ones – most people won't even notice it in everyday social conversation).

When the subjects are linked by expressions like *along with, in conjunction with, in collaboration* and *with as well as*, the main subject (underlined) determines whether the verb is singular or plural:

*Harry, along with his cousin, **runs** a small software company.*

*The two sisters, in collaboration with their younger brother, **make** documentaries for TV.*

Complex subjects (the risk of infections, pressures on the living wage)

Complications arise when the subject is a complex phrase with a mix of singular and plural elements. Here are two recently heard examples from TV and radio that have got themselves into a twist.

We are redefining what the value of things are.

When too many hospital beds are occupied, the risk of infections increase.

People often get confused by the nearest noun to the verb, in the first example the plural *things* and in the second example the plural *infections*, so these speakers have made the verb plural. But the main nouns in the underlined phrases (the headwords as they're sometimes called) are *value* and *risk*; the phrases *of things* and *of infections* simply specify what kind of value and what kind of risk we're talking about. *Value* and *risk* are both singular, so the verb should be *is* in both cases, not *are*. Another recent, similar BBC radio example was:

The unity of the 27 member states are important.

Unity is singular, so the verb should be *is*, not *are*. The next example also comes from a flagship BBC Radio 4 news programme. Here the opposite is the case, and verb should be *are*, not *is*.

Pressures on the living wage is only going to increase.

It is likely that the nearby singular noun *wage* is causing interference; it's also possible the speaker is thinking of *pressures on the living wage* as one single issue.

Problems with concord are common. You'll hear them regularly in the media even from so-called highly-educated speakers and they are endemic in business letters and emails.

Here's a (disguised) example from an email I received from a professional person who should have known better.

*We are confident that the data to which that formula **were** applied are accurate.*

It's the formula that was applied, not the data. So, *was* is correct, not *were*, unless the writer was insisting on using a regional dialect which has *were* as the third person singular past tense of *be*, which would be odd in such a formal sentence.

It could also be an (unlikely in this case) attempt to impress the reader that the writer knows that *data* is the plural form of *datum* (note the plural <u>are</u> *accurate*).

Tip: don't be fooled by the nearest noun to the verb. Look for the main noun in the phrase (the headword).

See also DATA

What-clauses as subject (what we need is more money)

This is about sentences like the following.

*What you need **is** more up-to-date software.*

*What I love **are** those nature documentaries. Some of the photography is amazing.*

We can see that, in general, the verb is singular or plural depending on what follows. However, what follows can also be viewed as a single event or idea, even though there's a plural noun involved.

*What we're seeing **is** more and more people doing all their business on mobile devices rather than on big, clunky old desktops.*

A singular verb or a plural verb would both be correct in this last example.

Agreement with *either ... or, neither ... nor, both ... and*

With *either ... or* and *neither ... nor*, use a singular verb. With *both ... and*, use a plural.

<u>Neither he nor his partner</u> **speaks** *Chinese, so they have to hope their clients are good at English.*

Either Suzie or Geoff **pops** *in to see her every day to make sure she's all right.*
Both Philip and Irene **are** *keen to join the group. What shall I tell them?*
This is a convention that is often disregarded, so don't be surprised to find plural verbs in all these cases.

Agreement with *neither of* and *none of*
In more formal writing or speaking, *neither of* is generally used with a singular verb.
I offered Karen and Leonard tickets for the show but neither of them **wants** *to go.*
But just the other day, a well-educated friend said about two people:
Neither of them **seem** *to know what's going on.*
I don't think anyone would even notice this in speech, apart from tiresome people like me who have trained one ear to listen to what people are saying and the other ear to how they say it. Now there's a confession that might lose me a few friends.
None of was traditionally held to be singular ('not one of') and so should take a singular verb, but that rule is widely ignored when it refers to a plural group of people or things, except in formal speaking and writing.
None of the stolen cars **was** *ever recovered.* (formal)
None of my friends ever **go** *to church.* (most frequently said)

Agreement with words like *majority, government, army*
This rather depends on how you look at groups of people and things, whether as one single mass, or as made up of separate, individual entities.
The army **has** *had its budget cut.* (a single mass)
The army **are** *furious about the new budget cuts.* (a collective of individuals)
All the government **are** *basically right wing.* (a collective of individuals)
The government **is** *split over the fracking issue.* (a single mass)

Here are two BBC radio examples:
*The Metropolitan Police **has** apologized to* [name removed]. (a single mass)
*Downing Street **are** listening*. (collective of individuals around the Prime Minister)
The next one is also from BBC radio, by the distinguished broadcaster John Humphrys, himself author of a well-received book on English usage[1]:
*A body that represents pharmacists **say** that funding rates* ...[etc.]
Here, the idea of a *body* being composed of a set of individuals has produced what would jar on many an ear and which looks slightly odd when written down. And that's the point: real-time speaking is full of things that might not be appropriate in writing. When we write, we can give more time and thought to our choices.
Purists probably won't like what I've just written, but unless you're in deep denial, you'll hear both types of agreement. Choose what sounds best for the situation.
See also AMOUNT OF or NUMBER OF, DATA, MEDIA, REFLEXIVE PRONOUNS (MYSELF, YOURSELF)

ALL and ALL OF

Both *all* and *all of* can be followed by the definite article (*the*), a possessive determiner (*my, your, his, her, its, our, their*), a demonstrative determiner (*this, that, these, those*) or a noun phrase (*Freda's books, the cars*). *All of* is by far the less frequent of the two:
All (of) our cabbages *were eaten by slugs.*
*They invited **all (of)*** George's relatives *to the surprise birthday party.*
*You can have **all (of)*** these old books *here; we were just going to throw them out.*

---
[1] Humphrys, J. (2005) *Lost For Words: The Mangling and Manipulating of the English Language*. London: Hodder & Stoughton.

ALL RIGHT or ALRIGHT

With the meaning of 'okay', it doesn't matter which one you use. Traditionalists think *alright* is somewhat non-standard; Fowler's 1926 *A Dictionary of Modern English Usage* said it should always be written as two words, *all right*. But don't worry yourself over it. And of course, if you mean 'all correct' then it is indeed two words, as in:
*They were difficult sums. Well done, you got them **all right**.*

ALL TOGETHER or ALTOGETHER

*Are you **all together** or do you want separate bills?* (in a group)
Altogether means 'totally/completely' or 'all things considered'.
*That comes to 57 pounds **altogether**. How would you like to pay?* (in total)
*It was **altogether** the craziest idea I've ever heard.* (all things considered)

ALTERNATE or ALTERNATIVE

This is complicated by American English, which uses *alternate* as an adjective where British English prefers *alternative*. Here's the conventional British version:
*You can drive into the city on **alternate** weekdays, depending on your number-plate.* (every other weekday)
*They were renovating the place so we had to find an **alternative** venue.* (a different one to use instead)
American English is quite happy with *alternate venue* in the second example.

A LOT and ALOT

Remember to write a space between *a* and *lot*:
***A lot** of people go to Croatia for their holidays these days.*
(Not ~~alot~~)

AMERICAN INFLUENCES
American and British English

Some people consider the influence of American English on British English to be an abomination and the term *Americanism* is sometimes said with the nose turned slightly upward. Not only is this disrespectful, since no variety of any language is more valid than any other, but the influence of global media is a reality and American English tends to dominate in global popular culture. American English is often highly creative and enriches the international English repertoire.

What is more, some aspects of American English have a long pedigree and reflect the British English of former times. Words and grammar that are sometimes thought of as new, trendy or sloppy American imports often turn out to be older than, or as old as, current British English forms. The use of *through*, as in *Monday through Friday* (it would have been *Monday to Friday* when I was a nipper), is attested back to the end of the 18th century. American usage that allows utterances such as *real good* instead of *really good* has its origins in Scottish English. The valedictory phrase *Enjoy!,* now quite common when addressed to one who is about to embark upon a potentially pleasant experience, is often thought of as an American import. It is often seen as representing a change from a transitive verb that must have an object (*enjoy your holiday, enjoy yourself*) to an intransitive verb that doesn't need one. In fact, intransitive uses of the verb *to enjoy* go back hundreds of years. Similarly, the American use of *pled* instead of *pleaded,* as in *She pled guilty,* goes back to at least the 16th century.

Transportation is a word with a long pedigree also going back to the 16th century. However, when it was a case of waiting for the bus that never came and then two came along, British English preferred to refer to *public transport*, while American English preferred *public transportation*. We have a grammatical grey squirrel here: more and more now, we hear *public transportation* in British English. Take your pick: adopt a grey squirrel or join the campaign to save the red.

Scots-Irish influences on the evolution of American English were significant historically and some examples of American English grammar reflect those influences (e.g. the dialect use of *whenever* instead of *when* in sentences such as *Whenever I was a child, we lived in Georgia*, heard in some southern US states).

American English grammar influencing British English and global English is often just a case of bringing it all back home.

American and British grammar: Some current differences

There are some differences between conventional standard British English grammar and standard American English grammar that you may come across. Here are some examples. Once again, these are in constant flux and you will hear both versions in British English and sometimes both in American:

British	American
at the weekend	*on the weekend*
be in a team	*be on a team*
I haven't seen her for 10 years	*I haven't seen her in 10 years*
Have they left already?	*Did they leave already?*
Have you got a pen?	*Do you have a pen?*
He fitted the profile perfectly	*He fit the profile perfectly*
We'd got back late	*We'd gotten back late*
A: I found my keys *B: Did you?*	*A: I found my keys* *B: You did?*

Recently, while I was browsing in a clothes shop that was in the midst of its post-Christmas sale, a young sales assistant told me that the jeans I was interested in were *not on sale*. I repressed my curmudgeonly instinct to reply *Oh, well, in that case no-one can buy them*. British English traditionally would have demanded *not in the sale* in this situation; *on sale* meant 'available for anyone to buy'. In American usage *on sale* refers to goods at a reduced price, and this has clearly worked its way into usage on this side of the Atlantic

American influences: Social routines

In former times, an informal British English greeting in the street was *Hi!* This has morphed into what one hears more and more now, American *Hey!* It's often then followed by a purely social (i.e. not medical) enquiry such as *How you doin'?* or *How are you guys?*, which then gets the reply *I'm/We're good!*, replacing the traditional *I'm/We're (very) well, thank you*. *Good* is lengthened and given a high-falling intonation, and you can almost hear the exclamation mark. Do such changes matter, or presage the imminent demise of polite society? Most certainly not. Grammar and social routines change and evolve.

American influences: Pronunciation

Because of America's influence on global media and culture, some words which had a conventional British English pronunciation (or which alternated between the two pronunciations given here) have shifted in recent years towards favouring their American equivalents. Examples include: re**search** (Br), **res**earch (Am), di**spute** (Br), **dis**pute (Am), Bagh**dad** (Br), **Bagh**dad (Am). The first syllable of *leverage* rhymes with *leave* in British English, but it is being increasingly replaced by the American pronunciation, which rhymes with *beverage*. And *schedule* with a *sh*-sound is definitely fighting a losing battle against *schedule* with a *sk*-sound.

You are nowadays likely to hear *enclave* pronounced in the broadcast media both in its traditional British English way (en-clave, where *en-* rhymes with *when*) and its American English pronunciation (on-clave, where *on-* rhymes with *gone,* but with a touch of pseudo-French nasality).

A young British-English-speaking waiter recently told me a dish contained *basil* (which he pronounced as rhyming with *hazel,* the American pronunciation). Watch out for that one.

And watch out for *airplane* replacing *aeroplane*; I think it might have already landed.

See also ACCOMMODATION, AROUND and ROUND, ALTERNATE or ALTERNATIVE, -CE OR -SE: NOUNS AND VERBS, GET, LIKELY, SHALL and WILL

AMOUNT OF or NUMBER OF

This seems to be a changing landscape, but here's the traditional view.

Traditionally, *amount of* is used with nouns we don't normally use in the plural (e.g. *furniture, information, rice, money, equipment*). They're called uncountable or mass nouns.

*That's a huge **amount of rice** for three people.*

*It's not worth spending a great **amount of time** over it.*

Number of was traditionally used for nouns in the plural.

*It's happened **a number of times** to people I know.*

***The number of deaths and injuries** has tripled over the last ten years.*

However, you'll often see and hear examples like this, and often with a plural verb.

The amount of cases of identity fraud <u>have</u> *increased a lot in the last few years.*

It's up to you how concerned you're prepared to get over this one, but always remember that people may judge you on what they consider to be correct or 'proper' grammar, and that what goes unnoticed in speaking can often stick out like a sore thumb in writing.

Subject-verb agreement with *number of* is worthy of note here. The expression *a number of* takes a plural verb:

A number of cases of internet bullying **have** led to tragic consequences.

The number of takes a singular verb:

The number of cases of bullying on the internet **has** increased dramatically.

*A number o*f is often used with *there are*, even though *a number* is singular:

There are a number of things we need to discuss.

ANACOLUTHIA

No, it's not a Russian Princess or a novel by Tolstoy. It means starting off a grammatical structure in one way then wandering off into a different structure before finishing the sentence.

This sort of thing can easily be a slip of the tongue that no-one will notice in real-time speaking but the one that always made me laugh was the announcement that advised passengers before take-off on a well-known budget airline:

Use of laptop computers may not be used till the fasten seatbelt sign has been switched off.

It was a recorded message that probably took a whole committee weeks to come up with. Have you ever tried 'using the use of' a laptop?

Anyway, the airline mended its ways, laptops increasingly became overtaken by tablets and smart phones and you won't hear that one any more. The moral of this story is don't wander off.

ANOTHER

This concerns an oddity I'm quite fond of. It's an oddity because,

while English uses lots of prefixes and suffixes, it only rarely drops other words into the middle of a word (it happens when you say something like *fan-flippin'-tastic*, or *abso-bloody-lutely*). What happens with *another* is illustrated in the following, heard recently on TV:
*The electron microscope has given scientists access to **a whole nother** world of research possibilities.*
This passes unnoticed in ordinary talk and would probably never appear in writing, but, listen out for it and you'll hear it from even so-called highly educated speakers, in both British and American English. It's like the process referred to in rhetoric when a compound word is split to let another word into the middle. This is known as *tmesis,* pronounced *t'MEEsis*/ˈtmiːsɪs/. Now that's definitely one to impress your friends with if you can say it.

ANY MORE or ANYMORE
Think of *any more* as question and negative equivalents of *some more*. It refers to numbers and quantities.
*Do you need **any more** chairs?*
*I can't eat **any more**, thanks, but it was delicious.*
Anymore just means 'no longer' or 'any longer'.
*They don't make film cameras **anymore**. They're all digital now.*
As usual, there's a complication: don't be surprised to see *any more* written as two words in examples like the one about cameras. A bit maddening, isn't it, just when you thought you'd got it sorted?

APOSTROPHES
What's an apostrophe and what's it for?
An apostrophe is written as a superscript comma ('). It has two main uses: to indicate possession and to show that something has been shortened. As with some other elements of grammar, conventions shift and change, and emails, texts and tweets are

usually less strict about apostrophes.

Possession, close association (Jack's coat, Denmark's economy)
The apostrophe is used to express a relationship of belonging or close association between two people or things, as in *Laura's coat, Krishnan's house, America's foreign policy, Ireland's capital, the ship's anchor*.

The thing to remember is that a plural noun has the apostrophe after the plural -s ending, as in *the list of members' names* (i.e. more than one member), *the boys' parents* (more than one boy). Some plurals are irregular; then you just add 's (*the children's menu, the men's toilets, a women's refuge*).

What about names ending in -s, like *James* or *Iglesias* or *Jones* or *Phyllis*? The same - just add 's: *James's car, Phyllis's desk*.

If you want to be ever so formal, you can <u>write</u> *King James' reign* but *King James's reign* is also okay. However, you'd probably want to <u>say</u> *King James's* when speaking. Some names like *Aristophanes* and *Archimedes* are a bit of a mouthful already and so it's easier to say *Aristophanes'* and *Archimedes'* than *Aristophanes's* or *Archimedes's* (especially after a couple of drinks).

Aristophanes' plays are the main source of what we know about the man himself.
What's Archimedes' principle? I've forgotten.

More than one possessor (Nick and Claire's house)
When two people or things are involved in the possession or relation of belonging referring to the same thing, it's only necessary to use one apostrophe.

We're invited to a party at <u>Nick and Claire's house</u>.
<u>Ron Carter and Mike McCarthy's</u> English grammar is a good read (we hope).

But you can separate out ownership by using more than one apostrophe in cases where the persons or things possessed are separate entities.

Mike's, Cynan's and Jake's voices are very different but they harmonise well when they sing (we're forever hopeful).

Apostrophe: Noun phrases (the woman in red's husband)
The *'s* goes at the end of a noun phrase. It's quite okay to say:
He's the woman who chairs our committee's husband.
In writing, especially formal writing, we might prefer an *of* construction:
He is the husband of the woman who chairs our committee.

Contractions (I'm Welsh, she's Scottish)
The apostrophe shows that something is a contraction (i.e. it has been shortened). Instead of saying *I am Welsh, we would love to, she is Scottish, they have left, he had arrived* and so on, we usually say *I'm Welsh, we'd love to, she's Scottish, they've left, he'd arrived.* In more formal writing, it's probably safest to use the long forms. There's a favourite school exercise-book howler. We often say *would've, could've* and *should've*, where the *'ve* has a similar pronunciation to 'of' but please don't write them as *would of could of* or *should of*. It would be less painful if you scratched your nails down the blackboard!

And don't believe that people during Queen Elizabeth I's reign or Jane Austen's time always spoke in long forms – that's just bad script-writing.

Some other examples of apostrophes indicating missing characters:
fish'n'chips, o'er the hills, three o'clock, '60s music, I moved here in '92
But only pedants still write *'phone, 'bye, 'bus* (*telephone, goodbye, omnibus*).

Apostrophe: *Who's* and *whose*
Don't mix up *who's* (who is/who has) and *whose* (to show possession). This is an easy mistake to make and mostly it involves using *who's* when it should be *whose*.

Who's *coming to dinner?* (who is)
*I don't know **who's** left this scarf here.* (who has)
Whose *coat is this?* (possession)
Daniel, ***whose*** *father was a seaman, also decided to go to sea.* (possession)

Apostrophe: Street names, signs, etc.

There's often a kerfuffle about street names, building names and other public signs without *'s*; there was one recently in Cambridge over *Scholars' Walk*. Cambridge City Council decided to do away with apostrophes in street names, which caused a rumpus. Mild controversy bubbles up now and then in my home village about our village hall which goes by the wonderfully socialist name of *The Peoples Hall*. (*People's?*)

In such cases, it looks as if there should be an apostrophe to show belonging or close association, as in *King George's wife*. Life is too short to worry a lot about this one, but if you want an explanation or justification for no apostrophe (NB I'm no apologist for Cambridge City Council), then think of a street name or building name like any other proper name or compound noun such as *Buckingham Palace* or *Downing Street*, which don't need *'s*, despite their close association with famous people and places. In fact, there are lots of cases of belonging and possession where English never uses *'s* and just prefers a good old compound noun.

*The **door handle** has come off.*
*The **team coach**, Charlie Wilson, was excellent.*
*I love polishing the **piano keys**; it sounds like experimental music.*

Oh, by the way, Cambridge City Council backed down and reversed its policy of no-apostrophe street signs. And it's not just Cambridge where this happens. Try doing an internet search on apostrophes in street signs to get a flavour for the strong feeling about this.

Apostrophe: *The 1920s, the 1840's, CD's, DVDs*

You don't need to use an apostrophe with the names of decades, but no one will arrest you if you do. The same applies to things like *a '70s/70s haircut, back in the '80s/80s*, but they'd certainly look a bit over the top with two apostrophes: *a '70's haircut* – hmmm... Similarly, you don't need an apostrophe with the plural of words like *CD* or *DVD*, but it happens because people find it odd to follow a group of capital letters by a small one:
CDs and DVDs are being overtaken by direct streaming of music and films.

Apostrophe: *Five minutes' walk*

What about *It's just five minutes' walk from here*? Conventionally, an apostrophe is used, but you'll see it without plenty of times. You could equally well write *It's just a **five-minute** walk from here* (which usually has a hyphen, but more about that under H).

If the number is just one, *'s* is used.

*It's just **an hour's** drive from the airport.*

Again, you could instead write *It's just a one-hour drive from the airport.*

Apostrophe: The greengrocer's plural

Apostrophes are not used to indicate a plural. Whatever you do, don't write *I love banana's*. That will just drive people bananas.

See also IT'S or ITS, ONES and ONE'S, YOU'RE and YOUR

AROUND and ROUND

Both *around* and *round* can be used as prepositions or adverbs.
*Francis Drake sailed **(a)round** the world in 1577-1580.* (preposition)
*I looked **(a)round** and saw someone running towards me.* (adverb)
However, my grammar-checker doesn't like it if I write *She lives round the corner from us* and wants me to write *around the corner*. This seems to be an American English influence. American English generally prefers *around*. Chuck Berry threw a spanner in the works

with his 1958 song entitled *Around and Around*, where we're told in the opening verse that the joint was *goin' round and round*, so there we have both forms cheek by jowl. While we're on music, the 19th century English folksong immortalised by the folk-rock band Steeleye Span in 1975 is most definitely *All Around my Hat*. The expression *all the year round* tends always to prefer *round*. But my grammar-checker is still not happy.

AS and LIKE

We could spend a lot of time on this one but the only area likely to get the purists hot under the collar is whether you should say:
*You should do **like** I did and lodge a formal complaint.*
or: *You should do **as** I did and lodge a formal complaint.*
*It looks **like** it's going to rain.*
or: *It looks **as if / as though** it's going to rain.*
Formal versions use *as* when a clause follows (e.g. *I did / it's going to rain*) and *like* when a noun or pronoun follows:
***Like** most people I know, I'm fed up with the commercialisation of Christmas.*
In informal speech, only people who don't deserve to be your friends will pull you up on the use of *like*.
***Like** me, you've probably got a lot to complain about.*
You must think I get my field-notes from the most miserable, whingeing people. Most of us spend more time talking about problems and negative things than nice, happy things. Bad news is good news.
Rebecca Hughes's 1996 book *English in Speech and Writing*, where she compares the official record of the British Parliament with the words that were actually uttered, has an example of an MP saying *... it will do the same for politics like it has done with football*. The official record changed *like* to *as*. Enough said.

AS LONG AS and SO LONG AS

Both of these can mean 'on condition that' or '(only) if'. They are genuine alternatives, so feel free to choose.

*You can go out **as/so long as** you're back by ten.*

In slightly more formal contexts, *provided/providing (that)* carry the same meaning.

See also PROVIDED AND PROVIDING (THAT)

BESIDE or BESIDES

Beside is a preposition meaning 'at the side' of or 'next to'.

*Come and sit **beside** me.*

Besides is most often an adverb meaning 'also' or 'what's more'.

*I'm too tired to go jogging. **Besides**, it's raining out there.*

It can also be used as a preposition meaning 'apart from' or 'in addition to'.

***Besides** playing the clarinet, she's pretty good on the piano.*

BETWEEN or AMONG

Generations of schoolchildren have been told that *between* should be used with two people or things, and *among* should be used when more than two are involved. Some grammars still stick to that. Many users of English happily ignore that rule.

But just for completeness, here's how it is supposed to work.

*Share this money **between** the two of you.*

*The dog had disappeared **among** the bushes.* (several or a lot of bushes)

And here's what you'll often actually hear.

*How can you share 100 pounds equally **between** three people?*

If you want to be formal, use the traditional rule. Otherwise, just say what comes naturally.

You can also say *amongst* instead of *among*, but *among* is about 20 times more commonly used in present-day English than *amongst*. Just for info.

BETWEEN YOU AND ME

You often hear people say: **Between you and I**, *she's not been very well lately.* The educated-standard form should be: **Between you and me**, *she's not been very well lately.*

Between you and I comes from old-fashioned school teachers telling children that *me* is an impolite word or is a sign of bad grammar. That's nonsense. *Between* is a preposition, just like *of, to, from, at, among*. Prepositions are followed by the object forms of the personal pronouns. The object forms are *me, you, him, her, us, them*. You wouldn't say *This is a present from I*; you'd say *This is a present from me*. You wouldn't say *Come and sit between I and David*; you'd say *Come and sit between me and David*.

But maybe we shouldn't get too hot under the collar; Shakespeare offers us both versions:

... *all debts are cleared* **between you and I,** ...
(Merchant of Venice, Act III, scene 2)
God above deal **between thee and me***!*
(Macbeth, Act IV, scene 3).

-CE or -SE: (PRACTICE, PRACTISE)

This concerns the spelling of some verbs and corresponding noun forms. The British English convention is *-se* for the verb, *-ce* for the noun

verb	noun
advise	advice
license	licence
practise	practice

Note also the verb *to prophesy* and the noun *a prophecy*

A complication stems from the fact that the compound noun *driving licence* (*-ce*) in British English is rendered as *driver's license* (*-se*) in American English, while the noun and verb forms of *practice* are both spelt with a *c* in American English.
And as if that wasn't enough, the noun *defence* (*-ce*, British) is *defense* (*-se*) in American English.

CAN, MAY and MIGHT

The issue here is one of formality. Only the most literal-minded (and wrong-headed) pedant would insist that in situations involving requests and permission, *can* refers to ability and *may* to permission.
Can *I join you? Yes, of course you **can**. Pull up a chair.*
May is far more formal:
May *I offer a suggestion, Chair? Yes, you **may**.*
If you want to be even more formal, *might* is also available:
Might *I propose an adjournment until we have more information?*
One of my peer reviewers of this book informs me that children who are taught good table manners often come out with funny things like *May you pass me the butter, please?* This is a kind of hypercorrection based on the notion that *may* is always more polite.

CAPITAL LETTERS

Capital, or upper case letters, were a lot more commonly used in former times. John Brightland's *A Grammar of the English Tongue* (1711) follows the convention of capitalising every noun. Brightland obviously disliked the practice but was himself trapped in it (or perhaps was being ironic at the reader's expense):
It is grown customary in Printing, to begin every Substantive* with a Capital, but 'tis unnecessary, and hinders that expressive Beauty and remarkable Distinction intended by the Capitals. (* noun)

In modern English, the first word of a sentence, the names of people and places, titles and initials denoting qualifications are capitalised:

*The founder was **Mr** George Carey, **MA**, who studied at **O**xford.*

Mount Everest, Lake Titicaca, Asia, Death Valley

The is usually written with a small letter in geographical names and the names of buildings and institutions:

the Thames, the Danube, the Amazon, the Antarctic, the Alps, the House of Commons, the British Museum

Abbreviations and personal initials use capital letters:

ITV, RSPB, P. G. *Wodehouse*

Languages and nationalities are capitalised:

Russian, Swahili, Bahasa Malaysia, Gaelic

The first and main words of the titles of books, poems, films, paintings, musical works and so on are normally capitalised, but minor words such as prepositions, conjunctions and articles are usually not in capitals:

<u>A Guest at the Feast</u>, *by Colm Tóibín*

<u>Dedham Lock and Mill</u>, *by John Constable*

The names of days, months and important days of the year are capitalised.

Tuesday, April, New Year's Day, Spring Bank Holiday

The names of the seasons (*spring, summer, autumn, winter*) are not capitalised.

The compass references *north, south, east* and *west* are not capitalised except when they are part of a proper noun (i.e. place names):

*It's a large town in the **south** of the country.*

*He lives in **Northern** Ireland.*

For the names of specific institutions or organisations, a capital letter is used. For references to such organisations in general, a capital letter is not needed:

She studied at Newcastle University from 2010-2013.
Is there a university in King's Lynn?

The internet used to be written with a capital letter (*the Internet*), but the small letter is steadily taking over as the web becomes an ordinary part of people's lives.

The pronoun *I* is capitalised (*Will I need a ticket?*), but it is very often written as a small letter in text messages and informal emails:

shall *i* pick u up 8.15?

In fact, a recent national newspaper advertisement for the charity Barnardo's used a small letter for the pronoun *I* throughout. Very i-catching.

CLICHÉS

Clichés are things that are said so often that they lose their originality and become tedious and sometimes irritating. If I hear another TV history, science or nature documentary that has the line *I'm X and I'm on my way to [place] to meet Y*, I'll throw something at the TV set.

Other irritations are *at this moment in time* (are there any other kinds of moments?), *going forward* and *at the end of the day*, which are heard so often in the media that they have become a sort of brain-dulling opiate.

Then there is *Let me be clear* or *Let's be clear*, which customarily prefaces an obfuscating response by a politician. Meanwhile, there are tiresome media commentators who refer to almost anything in politics as a *narrative* and everything that's going to happen in the run up to some important event as *ahead of* (*the summit, the talks*, etc.). Whatever happened to *before* or *prior to*? And why every set of events in someone's personal or public life has to be a *journey*, I do not know.

Do try to avoid clichés. Meanwhile, have a nice day.

COLON

A colon (:) can be used to introduce a list of people or things.

There are three types of clothing you must take with you on a hike: waterproofs, extra layers for warmth and headgear of some sort.

The subtitles and sub-headings of books and articles are often preceded by a colon.

English Grammar: Your Questions Answered

In the case of book and article titles and headings, usage varies as to whether the next word after the colon has a capital letter.

Some publishers use colons before quoted speech.

She looked at him angrily and said: 'Over my dead body!'

Colons are often used for times.

The flight departs at 09:20 and arrives at 11:30.

COMMA

Commas in lists (laptops, tablets and phones)

British English normally follows the convention of a comma after every item in a list except the last one, which usually has *and* before it.

Go into any family home in the evening and you'll find everyone glued to TVs, PCs, laptops, tablets and phones, often without exchanging a word.

In cases where there's another *and* in the environment, it's often helpful to use a comma along with *and* before the final item. Let me quote myself here, from the introduction to this book.

Then there are components like apostrophe 's, plural -(e)s, past tense -ed and present participle -ing, and symbols such as commas, full stops and question marks.

So, that's straightforward.

Would that life were that simple. American English always prefers a comma before the *and*. Some British publishers ask their authors to put them in too. It's known as the Oxford comma or the serial comma.

Commas with adjectives (a long, blue, silk dress)

When more than one adjective is used before a noun, we normally separate them with a comma after each one except for the final one:

An elegant, long, blue, silk dress

However, when an adjective forms part of a compound noun or is very closely associated with the noun, commas are not used:

We saw a beautiful red kite. (i.e. the bird; not: *a beautiful, red kite*, which might suggest a kite on a string)

A gorgeous, full-bodied, aromatic Italian red wine

Commas: More than one main clause (she sings and plays the guitar)

When there are two main clauses linked by words like *and, but* and *or*, we don't need a comma.

She sings and plays the guitar.

With more than two main clauses, it's just like any list: commas before all but the last clause.

He sings in a choir, he belongs to a chess club, he's a brilliant squash-player and he speaks fluent Norwegian. He makes me feel like a complete waste of space.

You can have a starter and a main course, you can have two starters and no main course but you can't have two main courses. Otherwise, they're pretty flexible.

Commas after subordinate clauses (if you're driving, take the M5)

Subordinate clauses are clauses that don't make much sense on their own. They need to be attached to a main clause to make a full sentence or to a context where it's obvious to the listeners/readers what they mean. Examples are clauses starting with *if, when, as, because, before, after.*

When a subordinate clause comes before the main clause, it's normal to use a comma.

When you've finished, we can take the dog for a walk.
If it makes life simpler, Gregori can book into a B&B.

When a subordinate clause comes after a main clause, we don't need one.

Will you look over this email *before I send it off?* Tell me if there are any grammatical howlers in it.

She bumped into her ex-husband *as she was coming out of Victoria Station.*

Commas before and after embedded clauses (we could, if you prefer, leave earlier)

That's a bit of a mouthful, but all it means is that, *when you're doing what I'm doing now and inserting a subordinate clause in the middle of a main one,* you should separate it off with commas.

We could, *if it is more convenient,* bring the meeting forward by a day or two.

Commas and linking words and phrases (it could cost a lot more, however)

It's normal to use commas to separate off linking words and phrases like *however, therefore, nevertheless, on the other hand, as a result* and so on.

Families are welcome. *However,* we cannot allow children to approach the bonfire unless accompanied by a responsible adult.

She's your customer and you've always dealt with her. I will, *therefore,* respect your decision on how to proceed.

This convention is not always strictly adhered to, especially in emails, blogs, text messages and the like. U can there4 ignore it if u want.

Commas around noun phrases in apposition (Jim, the eldest son, is in prison)

Apposition is when you have two noun phrases referring to the same person or thing. Usage varies, with more formal contexts favouring commas. Sometimes, commas help to clarify things, so here are some tips.

My sister Mary worked for years as a librarian. (doesn't necessarily tell you how many sisters I have and it may not be relevant)

My sister Mary worked for years as a librarian. My other sister was in the army. (aha!)

My sister, Mary, was always cleverer than me at school. (the commas suggest I just have one sister)

If you say these out loud, the commas imply momentary pauses each side of *Mary*.

It's a bit like the section on Commas and relative clauses. The commas tend to bracket added information which can be removed without making the sentence cryptic or making it difficult to know who or what is being referred to.

His first novel, The Queen Never Came to Tea, was an immediate hit.

But, as usual, watch out for variations. What matters most is making your meaning clear and unambiguous.

No comma between subject and verb (the person who did it was drunk)

So many people break this convention that I'm probably fighting a losing battle on this one. Here are the kinds of examples I'm referring to. Subjects are underlined.

<u>The person who broke the windows</u>, was a disgruntled ex-employee of the firm.

<u>That she knew what was happening all along</u>, is obvious.

Neither of these needs a comma. We would not use a comma after a simpler subject such as *she* or *he* or *Diana Stevens*, so don't use one just because the subjects are long phrases or clauses.

No comma between *be* and its complement (the problem is that ...)

A complement is different from an object. Complements come after verbs like *be, become, seem, look, smell, taste* (*she's <u>a</u>*

lawyer, I've become less tolerant of hypocrites in my old age, it looks/smells/tastes pretty awful). When the complement is a *that*-clause or an infinitive clause, the temptation is to use a comma before it. Don't. You're just wearing out your keyboard. Here are two examples of unnecessary commas:

The problem is, that not everyone in the village is on email, especially some older residents. (*that*-clause)

Their strategy seems to be, to wait until things have settled down a bit. (infinitive clause)

But, as is so often the case, history confounds us. Lindley Murray, in his influential grammar of 1795, tells the reader under 'rule xvii' that a comma *should* be used in sentences with infinitive clauses after *be*:

The most obvious remedy is, to withdraw from all associations with bad men.

Many books from previous centuries are hirsute with commas and other punctuation that would seem excessive today. Some of the commas in this typical extract from Laurence Sterne's *The Life and Opinions of Tristram Shandy, Gentleman* (1759-1767), especially those which accompany dashes, now seem unnecessary:

I must here inform you, that this servant of my uncle Toby's, who went by the name of Trim, had been a corporal in my uncle's own company,—his real name was James Butler,—but having got the nick-name of Trim, in the regiment, my uncle Toby, unless when he happened to be very angry with him, would never call him by any other name.

(Chapter 1.XXX)

Old grammars and the literature of former times are a constant reminder that yesterday's norms are often today's jealously-guarded traditions for some, fossils and oddities for others, and tomorrow's howlers.

Commas separating off adverbial phrases (I love cakes, especially sponge cakes)

Adverbial phrases that comment on the whole clause or sentence are often separated off by commas. In speech, there is typically a brief pause where the comma is.

Some present-day grammars are completely dotty, <u>especially those by grammarians who still think English should follow the rules of Latin</u>.
<u>For what it's worth</u>, my inclination would be to cancel the whole thing.

Commas and vocatives: People directly addressed (Julia, come here, please)

When written, the names of people directly addressed are usually separated off by commas.

Please, Richard, don't be offended by what I'm about to tell you.
Irene, could you come and hold on to the dog for a minute?

See also RELATIVE CLAUSES (THE GIRL WHO BROKE THE WINDOW)

COMPARE TO and COMPARE WITH

Traditional usage was that *compare to* meant 'to say that something is similar to' or 'to liken'.

*She upset him by **comparing** his garden **to** a scrapyard.* (saying his garden was like a scrapyard)

Compare with meant simply to examine more than one person or thing to see if there are similarities or differences.

*If we **compare** Portuguese **with** Spanish, we see many similarities but enough differences to constitute them as separate languages.*

This traditional rule is not held to hard and fast, especially in the expression *compared to/with*, where both are common.

***Compared to/with** my old car, this one uses far less petrol.*

If you like the traditional rule, go with it; otherwise, don't worry.

COMPARATIVES (BIGGER, EASIER)
Comparative adjectives and adverbs (bigger, worse, more slowly)
Comparatives are used to compare two people or things or two situations.
*Geoff is **taller than** me.*
*His latest film is even **worse than the last one**.*
*She always speaks **more slowly** when she's tired.*
*Who was **the better** speaker, Jan Cullingworth or Ailsa Ward?*
In examples like this last one, where two people are compared, the comparative is the more formally correct, but people often use the superlative instead, which, strictly speaking, is used when singling out a person or thing from a group of more than two:
*Which is **the best** knife to cut the bread, this one or the other one?*
There's nothing new in this; it's not some latter-day corruption of the high standards set by the 18th century prescriptive grammarians. William Bullokar, some 430 years ago, in his *Pamphlet for Grammar*, at the section on comparatives, concedes:
... though we English use the superlative also when we compare but two things together. (modernised spelling and orthography)
Note that in *Geoff is taller than me*, above, we say *me*, not *I*. If, through some dark memory of being told off at school, *me* sticks in your throat, you can use *I* (or *he, she, we, they*, as the situation demands) by adding a verb:
*Geoff is taller **than I am**.*
*He achieved more **than she did**.*
Comparisons with *as ... as, not as ... as, not so ... as*
As with comparative adjectives and adverbs, the object forms of the personal pronouns are used.
*He went to university and his brother's just **as clever as him** but he didn't want to have to study.*
*He's not **as tall as her**.*
If your sense of symmetry is offended by the object pronouns, you

can salvage your dignity by continuing with a verb:
*He's not **as tall as she is**.*
Comparisons with *not so... as* are far less common than those with *not as ... as*.
*It turned out to be **not so far as** we thought and we were there in less than an hour.*

Comparisons with *that of*
That of is used in comparisons instead of repeating a noun:
*Her salary is equivalent to **that of** a university lecturer.* (i.e. equivalent to the salary of ...)
This can be expressed less formally with a possessive 's:
*Her salary is equivalent to **a university lecturer's**.*
In very informal talk, it is likely to go unnoticed if you say:
*Her salary is equivalent **to a university lecturer**.*
However, a purist would object to the comparison between a salary and a lecturer, rather than a comparison of two salaries.
That of is used after expressions such as *the same as, similar to, different from/to, greater/less than, like* and *comparable to/with*.
See also SUPERLATIVE

CONTINUOUS and CONTINUAL
Continuous means that something happens without any break or interruption.
*It looks better if you can show **continuous** employment on your cv without any unexplained gaps.*
Continual means something goes on and on but there may be interruptions or brief intermissions.
*Good software is subject to **continual** refinement during its lifetime.*
The corresponding adverb forms are *continuously* and *continually*.
*We worked **continuously** for 12 hours and were exhausted. We didn't even stop for a meal.*

*I'm **continually** amazed by how many people I see using mobile phones when driving.*

CONTRACTIONS

I hope this section won't be too laboured. Contractions are when short forms of verbs are used, as in *I'm okay, Joe's here, she'd love it, we've eaten, it isn't ready, they hadn't heard*, etc.

They project informality and therefore should be used with caution in formal writing. But if you want to project friendliness they are a good way of using the grammar. An official information leaflet from the UK Driver and Vehicle Licensing Agency (DVLA to most of us) laying out the rules pertaining to passing on vehicle tax when you sell or give away a vehicle contains *can't, it's, you'll, you're, you've* and *we're*. This is clearly designed to make the reader feel comfortable and cared for (before you're taken to court for breaking the rules) and is to be applauded as a break with the stuffiness of much official bureaucracy.

Don't confuse *you're* (*you are*) and *your* (possessive– *Is this your pen?*); this has crept into emails and text messages, where *your* often serves both meanings:

*I hope **you're** feeling better.* (Not ~~your~~)
***Your** new job seems to be keeping you busy.*
And don't confuse *were, we're* and *where*:
*They **were** tired.* (past tense of *they are tired*)
***We're** going out tonight.* (present tense of *be: We are going out*)
***Where** are you working these days?* (enquiring about a place)
Finally, remember to use the apostrophe in contractions, otherwise *we'll* becomes *well*, and, by curious analogy, *I'll* becomes *ill*.

See also Apostrophe: I'm Welsh, she's Scottish, Apostrophe: who's and whose, THERE, THERE'S, THEIR and THEIRS, YOU'RE and YOUR

CONTRIBUTE, DISTRIBUTE (PRONUNCIATION)

The pronunciation of these varies as to where the stress falls, whether on the middle or beginning of the word.

Stress on the middle of the word:

conTRIBute diSTRIBute

Stress at the beginning of the word:

CONtribute DIStribute

Both pronunciations are widely used and acceptable but online dictionaries by major publishers currently tend to favour stress on the middle of the word.

COUNTRIES

This concerns whether we use the definite article (*the*) in front of country names, and it's a bit of a mess, to be honest. Conventions have changed over the years and the definite article is now being used less and less. Formerly, people referred to *The Ukraine, The Gambia, The Lebanon* and one or two other countries in like manner. Most people now say *Ukraine, Gambia* and *Lebanon*.

The following have kept a stronger hold on their definite article: *The USA (The United States of America), The Netherlands, The Philippines, The Czech Republic, The Democratic Republic of the Congo*.

The United Arab Emirates is the name given on that country's official website, but on the British government's official travel advice website, it loses the definite article in its main heading but retains it in the accompanying text and the same applies to *(the) Netherlands* and *(the) USA*.

All countries on the United Nations list of member states web page are named without the article, except for *The former Yugoslav Republic of Macedonia*.

And what of *The United Kingdom*? I've lost count of the number of times recently I've heard it on the BBC used without the definite article in economic, political and sporting contexts.

CREATIVE WORD-FORMATION
Creative suffixes (Irangate, workaholic)
Suffixes are endings added to words that change their meaning or function. For example, -*ment* gives us nouns from verbs (e.g. *excitement, containment, judgement*), while -ful often indicates an adjective (*hateful, thankful, beautiful*). Some elements of words are used as if they were suffixes, often to great creative and humorous effect. From the word *alcoholic*, referring to an addiction to alcohol, other types of addiction have been given names. Examples include: *shopaholic, workaholic, chocaholic, blogaholic, textaholic, tweetaholic*.

Similarly, after the Watergate scandal in the USA in the 1970s, public scandals and controversies are often referred to using -*gate* as a suffix, such as *Climategate, Irangate* and recently in the UK when a leading supermarket chain threatened to stop selling the food product Marmite, *Marmitegate*. At the time of writing, *Wikipedia* offers a breath-taking list of -*gate* scandals.

Other creative uses of suffixes include *an anded couple* (for example, two TV presenters always mentioned in the same breath but who are not romantically related to each other) and of course the ubiquitous *selfie*.

Back formations (liaise, babysit)
English is a wonderfully flexible organism. Words can hop around from one word-class to another, they can change their shape like mimic octopuses and can acquire new meanings, constantly evolving to suit their environment.

Back formations are an example of this flexibility. By removing suffixes, or what look like suffixes, new versions of words can be formed. Here are some examples where verbs have been created from nouns:

babysitter – to babysit
bulldozer – to bulldoze

curator – to curate
head-hunter – to headhunt
liaison – to liaise
proofreader – to proofread

An interesting example of shortening a word that has left the population divided is that some people say *conflab* when they mean an informal chat to resolve some matter, while others prefer *confab*. Both are a shortened form of *confabulation* and the letter *l* seems to have migrated to a position after the *f* in *conflab*. *Confab* has the longer history and is by far the more frequently used of the two, but *conflab* is attested as far back as the mid-19th century.

Conversion (a big ask)
In the case of conversion, a word simply changes to another grammatical class.
*That's a big **ask**.* (*ask* changes from verb to noun)
***Text** me tomorrow to remind me.* (*text* changes from noun to verb)
*Who's going to **chair** the meeting?* (*chair* changes from noun to verb)
[TV historian about to put on safety goggles before firing a medieval cannon] *Time to **safety** up!* (*safety* changes from noun to verb)
Recently, a well-known author of whodunnits referred in a TV interview to a typical twist where the reader thinks they know who committed the foul crime, then suddenly, someone *alibis* the prime suspect. *Alibi* began life as an adverb (from the Latin meaning 'in another place'), then by the mid-18th century it had morphed to a noun and now this latest example sees it used as a verb.

Words can also simply change their meaning or add a new sense to their meaning to adapt to new social and technical realities. A *mouse* was once a rodent, now it's also a gadget for manipulating your computer. In my teens, *hipsters* were trousers that hung from the hip; now they're a type of middle-class person who is super-trendy.

Blends (smog, brunch)

English is perpetually creative. Bits of existing words and expressions can blend together to form new words and expressions to respond to new social and environmental conditions, for example s*moke + fog = smog, breakfast + lunch = brunch.*

In the 18th century, Horace Walpole coined the term *gloomth* (*gloom + warmth*) to evoke the atmosphere of great Gothic buildings. Lewis Carroll's creativity with words included his fabulous creature *The Frumious Bandersnatch*; he explained *frumious* as a blend of *fuming* and *furious*. In the late 19th century, the term *electrocute* (*electric + execute*) was coined in the USA.

In this century, *Grexit* and *Brexit* (*Greek + exit, British + exit*) were coined to refer to Greece's potential, and the UK's actual, exit from the European Union. Those who supported Brexit became known as *Brexiters* or *Brexiteers*. After the UK referendum vote to leave the EU in 2016, those who had voted to remain in the EU, known as *remainers*, but who continued to be vocal in their stance against the vote to leave, were branded *remoaners* (*remain + moaners*).

While Wi-Fi technology and hot-spots are ubiquitous in the UK, at the time of writing, some rural areas still suffer from slow internet connections and poor or no mobile phone signals. To describe such areas, *not-spots* was coined as an opposite of *hot-spots*.

Other recent blends include: *vlog* (*video + blog*), *malware* (*malicious + software*), *labradoodle* (*Labrador + poodle*), *webinar* (*web + seminar*).

CRITERION/CRITERIA, PHENOMENON/PHENOMENA

In each case, the *-on* ending is singular and the *-a* ending is plural.

An interesting phenomenon / a range of interesting phenomena
The single most important criterion / three essential criteria
You will often hear the plural forms (*criteria, phenomena*) used for singular and plural, and it may be that the singular forms are a threatened species.

DASHES

A dash is written like a long hyphen – use it with care. It suggests a pause (if you read the previous sentence out loud, you will probably pause briefly and take a breath at the dash).
Dashes can be used like brackets, to put something into parenthesis or apposition:
Dublin – Ireland's bustling capital city – became a popular destination for stag and hen parties.
A dash can also carry the meaning 'from-to' with days, dates and times:
Open Mon—Fri, 09:00—17:00
Headings and sub-headings often use dashes when the main text continues on the same line:
Tuesday 17 July – pick up your vehicle from our main depot at the airport
Tuesday 24 July – return your vehicle to our city centre depot in Bristol

DATA

Dictionaries sometimes give *day-ta* as the pronunciation; sometimes they give both *day-ta* and *daa-ta*. During my academic career, I heard *day-ta* more often among my British colleagues.
Strictly speaking *data* is a plural noun (singular: *datum*). Some people use a plural verb after it; some use a singular.
*The data **were** checked three times, and each time, minor errors were spotted.*

*All the old data **was** lost when the hard drive crashed.* A BBC radio commentator, obviously uncertain about the pronunciation, hedged his bets and referred to *dayta centres* then in the same breath changed it to *daata centres*. You could almost hear the forward slash between the words. My advice: take your pick.

DEFINITE(LY)
Just don't spell it *definate* or *definately*. And for the adverb form, one of my reviewers tells me she often sees *defiantly* these days. That's probably people's spell-checkers being too clever for their own good.

DIFFERENT TO, FROM, THAN
Many a word has been written on this issue. *Different from* is overall the most frequently used of the three alternatives.
*The landscape of that part of Turkey **is different from** that of the rest of the country.*
Different to is often preferred in speaking.
*Iris claims it was a civilised meeting but that's **different to** what I remember.*
Different than is generally considered to be American English; one of Bob Dylan's early songs contained the line *I ain't different than anyone* (*I Shall Be Free No. 10*, 1964). However, British English speakers sometimes use *different than* when it is followed by a clause (underlined here):
*He looks very **different than** when I last saw him. He's aged a lot.*
Different from or *different to* would also do just as well in this last example.
H. W. Fowler, in his *A Dictionary of Modern English Usage* (1926) dismissed the idea that *different* could only be followed by *from* as a *superstition*. Well said, Henry W.

DOUBLE IS (THE THING IS IS ...)

This is one that applies to speech. I don't think anyone would write it, but keep your ears open for it. It affects expressions like *the problem/question/thing/trouble is*:

*The question **is is**, why should we have to grit our own street when we pay the County Council to do it?*

This double use of *is* can be considered evidence of 'chunking', where expressions like *the question is* have the status of frozen routines or idioms, with no internal grammar. For the speaker, the first *is* doesn't count as a verb, so the sentence needs a proper verb, the second *is*.

To the best of my knowledge, the phenomenon was first reported fully in the academic literature in 1988, where the researcher noted that the two *is* are spoken in quick succession[2].

Not one to cause sleepless nights; just one to be aware of. It may not always be appropriate, especially in very formal situations.

DOUBLE NEGATIVES

Double negatives: When best not to use them (she hasn't got no money)

Although many dialects are quite happy with sentences like the following ones, the standard varieties which act as a sort of common coinage where English is used generally disapprove of them.

Non-standard/dialectal: *I **don't** want **nothing** to do with it.*

Standard: *I **don't** want **anything** to do with it.*

Non-standard/dialectal: *She **hasn't** got **no** money.*

Standard: *She **hasn't** got **any** money.*

Double negatives for emphasis with adjectives (not unreasonable)

Adjectives can be negated using prefixes like *un-* and *im-* (e.g.

---

[2] McConvell, P. (1988) *To be* or double *be*? Current changes in the English copula. *Australian Journal of Linguistics* 8 (2): 287-305.

unreasonable, impossible). For stylistic emphasis, these can be used with *not* to create a positive meaning in rather formal contexts.
*The demand for a public enquiry is **not unreasonable**, given the circumstances.*
*If this happens, street riots would be a **not implausible**, albeit disastrous, consequence.*

Other kinds of double negative (she's not here, I don't think)
Some kinds of double negative pass unnoticed in everyday speaking. Here are a couple of types you will hear on a regular basis.
*It's worth getting one. They're **not** that expensive, I **don't** think.*
If we reverse the clauses in the second sentence, one of the negatives disappears.
*It's worth getting one. I **don't** think they're that expensive.*
Here's another type you hear quite frequently.
*I **wouldn't** be surprised if they **didn't** split up. They're always bickering.*
A more strictly standard version would be *I wouldn't be surprised if they split up.*
Here's the type I like best. I couldn't resist writing this down as soon as I heard it. A and B are two speakers in conversation (okay, they were me and my wife):
A: I don't think we'll see much wildlife today.
*B: **Not** without binoculars we **won't**.*
So, two negatives don't always make a positive. The 18th-century grammarian, Robert Lowth, said: *Two negatives in English destroy one another.* Applying that kind of logic to everyday language use is unreliable.

DUE TO and OWING TO
People often worry about this one because they can't quite

remember what they were taught at school. They only remember that the teacher said it was a ghastly mistake if you used the wrong one. For my generation, that kind of rule belonged to the days when grammar, like television, was only available in black and white. Nowadays, the picture is more nuanced, but for those who want the traditional rule, here it is.

Owing to is a complex preposition which is always followed by a noun phrase.

Owing to *the bad weather, the village picnic has been postponed till next weekend.*

Due is an adjective that happens to be followed by *to*. It is used after the verb *to be*:

The delay **was due to** *a signalling failure further down the line.*

That's what we were taught at school, but be prepared to hear and see *due to* used in the first example and *owing to* used in the second. Your friends won't stop going out with you if you swap them round in conversation.

DUNNO, GONNA, GOTTA, WANNA

These forms are shortened versions, respectively, of *don't know, going to, got to* and *want to*. In the past they were confined to literary uses when attempting to capture the flavour of everyday casual speech. While they would be out of place in formal writing, they are very useful in contexts such as text messaging and tweeting as they are both economical and informal.

Listen to UK parliamentary debates (the real, live ones broadcast on radio and TV and online, not the cleaned-up versions in the official record); you will regularly hear MPs saying *gonna*, though they might never admit to it.

EACH OTHER and ONE ANOTHER

These are used to refer to reciprocal actions. The conventional

rule is that *each other* involves two subjects, while *one another* involves more than two.
*Jo and Hilary hate **each other**.* (Jo hates Hilary and Hilary hates Jo.)
*The committee members were always criticising **one another**.* (more than two people are involved)
This distinction is often ignored and few people would get on their high horse nowadays if they heard an adult address two squabbling children and say:
*Stop it, you two! Be nice to **one another**!*

EITHER and NEITHER
There are two pronunciations: eye-ther and nye-ther (same sound as in *sci-fi*) or eether and neether (same sound as is *bee's-knees*). British English tends to prefer the sci-fi versions; American English generally prefers the bee's-knees versions.
Me neither (pronounced in the American way) seems to be becoming more frequent in British English these days. Old fogeys like me grew up saying *Nor me* if someone said *I don't like Mondays*. Posh old fogeys grew up saying *Nor I*. There's a fair sprinkling of outraged reaction on the web to *Me either* (*me-eether*) being used in the same situation, so if you don't want to upset anyone, that's one to avoid.
Anyway, as far as the basic pronunciation goes, take your pick. Either will do.

ELLIPSIS (POSTMAN BEEN YET?)
Ellipsis means leaving out something that is normally considered to be required by the rules of grammar. I say 'normally' because, most of the time, people understand one another perfectly well in context even when messages are extremely brief, and do not feel that anything has been 'left out':
Finished? (Have you finished?)

Haven't had time to sort out the plumber yet, I'm sorry. (I haven't had time…)
You going to the film on Saturday? (Are you going …?)
Postman been yet? (Has the postman been yet?)
This kind of ellipsis is often called situational ellipsis, because the situation provides enough context for even very short utterances to be fully understood. The less contextual support there is (e.g. in a written document that will be read at a different time and place from when it was created), the more fully elaborated the grammar needs to be.

Sometimes, the sentence itself can provide enough clues by using parallel structures:
The main streets were a blaze of lamps and neon signs, the back streets a labyrinth of dark lanes. (understood to mean that the back streets *were* a labyrinth of dark lanes)
Richard Whately's *Elements of Rhetoric* (1828, quoted here from p.28 of the 1861 edition) contains a nice example of parallel structures:
… it is understood that correct use is not founded on Grammar, but Grammar on correct use. (understood to mean that grammar *is founded* on correct use)

ENDINGS IN -WARD or -WARDS (TOWARD[S])

The preposition *toward(s)* and the adverbs *backward(s), downward(s), forward(s), homeward(s), inwards, onward(s), outwards* and *upward(s)* present a choice whether to use the *-s* ending or not.

Backwards is far more common than *backward* as an adverb.

The adverb *forward* is far more common than *forwards*. The fixed expression *going forward* (meaning 'from here on') is extremely common in business English and in journalistic style, though it is infrequent in everyday social conversation.

Towards is more common than *toward* in British usage, though both are acceptable.
*She turned **toward(s)** the crowd and spoke.*
The same applies to *downwards, inwards, onwards, outwards* and *upwards*, with the *-s* ending being more common:
*We found a footpath leading on **downward(s)**, away from the peak.*
*They continued **onward(s)** until they saw some cottages.*
In the case of *homeward(s)*, the two forms are more equally distributed.
When they function as adjectives, the *-s* ending is not used:
*There was a **downward** trend in exports last year. **Inward** investment also suffered.*
*My **homeward** journey was far less stressful than the **outward** one.*

ESPECIALLY and SPECIALLY

Especially means 'particularly' or 'above all'.
*New England is wonderful, **especially** in the autumn.*
Specially is used when referring to a specific or unique purpose of something.
*The company makes office chairs **specially** designed for those who suffer from back problems.*
The confusion may come from the fact that, in informal speaking, *especially* often sounds like *specially*. The difference is more important in writing.

EVERY DAY and EVERYDAY

As two words, *every day* is an adverb or noun phrase.
*That sort of thing happens **every day**.* (adverb phrase)
***Every day** seems to get harder and harder.* (noun phrase)
Everyday is an adjective.
***Everyday** language is quite different from the formal language of legal texts.*

53

EXCLAMATION MARK

Exclamation marks are used after words and phrases that express immediate strong emotional reactions. The American English term is *exclamation point*.

Wow! Well, blow me down with a feather! I never thought I'd see you at the gym.

They are also used after what grammarians call exclamatives. These are typically clauses that look like questions but they aren't really; they're just strong statements.

Have I got news for you!
My God, did she make a fool of herself last night!

Exclamatives can also be constructed with *what*:

Thank you! What a kind person you are!

A traditional way of exclaiming using *how* has been overtaken by a different form in recent years. Instead of what was most common, i.e. a straightforward statement structure:

*How annoying **it is** when people drop litter on the beach!*

Nowadays, exclamations with *how* are frequently formed like a question:

*He wants to go and live in a tree. How crazy **is that**!*

There's also a tendency to use exclamation marks everywhere just to impress people that what you've got to say is newsworthy or very important. I'd strongly advise against it! It really gets on my nerves!

Some typefaces will allow you to produce a symbol which goes by the wonderful name of *interrobang*, a combination of question mark and exclamation mark (‽), designed to express the questioning and exclaiming functions simultaneously.

FARTHER/-EST or FURTHER/-EST

When referring to distance, either one is possible.

*How much **further/farther** is it to the hostel?*

The **farthest/furthest** she ever travelled from her village was a day trip to the seaside. But that's how it was in those days.
When referring to more abstract meanings, *further* is the one to use.
Further to my email of 3rd March, I can now confirm that we can come to fit the bathroom tiles on Monday 16th.
Further discussions will be held before a final decision is made.
Overall, *further* and *furthest* are far more frequently used than *farther* and *farthest*, so the 'u' forms are a safe bet.

FIRST(LY), SECOND(LY)

First and *firstly* can both be used to introduce a sequence of points or topics. Writers and (formal) speakers often use *first*, even when they follow it by *secondly, thirdly*, etc. *Firstly, secondly, thirdly* have a more formal ring to them than *first, second, third*. *Lastly* is generally preferred to *last*.
First(ly), let me thank you for your kind donation; it was most generous of you. **Secondly**, I wondered if you would be prepared to talk to our group about your own experience in the field? [intervening text] **Lastly**, may I ask you to complete the attached Gift Aid form, which...
When referring to a sequence of events in time, *first* is preferred to *firstly*.
Aedile: List to your tribunes. Audience: peace, I say!
Coriolanus: **First**, *hear me speak.*
(Shakespeare: *Coriolanus* Act III, Scene 3)
In speech, we often list different points using *A, B* and *C*:
Two reasons why I'm not going, **A** *I'm a bit short of cash and* **B** *I don't like coach outings anyway.*
People will tolerate up to *C*, but don't drone on to *F, G* and *H*; by that time, their concentration will have wandered.

FULL STOP

The full stop (or *period* as it's called in American English) is used to mark the end of sentences. It is also used to show that a word has been shortened by omitting letters up to and including the last letter of the word:

Prof. Carter will see you at 2.30pm. (Professor)
Phelan and Co. – your local estate agent (Company)
This book is by P. G. Wodehouse. (Pelham Grenville)

When the last letter of the word is retained, a full stop is not needed; however, American English generally prefers one.

Dr Wilson is on holiday this week. (Doctor)
St Andrew's Church is about to celebrate its 800th anniversary. (Saint)

Some sets of initials, especially longer ones, look better without full stops. When writing someone's academic qualifications after their name, full stops are often not used:

*Chairperson: Ellen Grimshaw **MA, PhD***
*Dr Zenab Allewar **FRSA** will give this year's guest lecture.* (Fellow of the Royal Society of Arts)

A full stop is sometimes used for effect when strictly speaking it doesn't mark the end of a sentence. This is common in advertising, evoking a friendly, conversational style of address to the unwitting victim.

*We have some fabulous reductions for this week only. **W**hich is why you should visit our website right away.*

GAOL and JAIL

This is purely a spelling issue. Both spellings have a very long history but it looks as if *jail* has won the hearts of the people. *Gaol* has shown a sharp decline in use since the 1950s in British English, while *jail* has been the preferred spelling in American English for centuries.

GET
What you may have learnt at school
When I was a kid, we sometimes had to do exercises where we had to substitute more elegant words instead of *get*. Overuse of *get* was considered a bit 'common' (i.e. lower-class, not 'common' in the sense I use it in this book, meaning 'very frequently used'). We struggled to say things *like purchase a newspaper, obtain a job, grow dark, alight from the bus* and so on, which would have guaranteed to get us beaten up by louts from rival schools if we ever uttered them in public.

The bad reputation of *get* persists, and there may be arguments for not overusing it in formal writing, but then that same argument would apply to *vicissitude* and *jejune*; good style often depends on varying one's words. In everyday speech, we can get by fine using *get* as often we like. I've even got (gotten?) used to the now ubiquitous *Can I get a regular latte?* in cafes and coffee shops, where I still want to say *Can I have a regular latte?*

Past participle (got or gotten)
James Greenwood's *The Royal English Grammar* of 1737 gives both *got* and *gotten* as past participles of *get*. Later, Robert Lowth, Lord Bishop of Oxford and arbiter of good grammar in the 18th century, rails against the use of *got* instead of the more desirable *gotten* as the past participle of *get*: *This abuse has been long growing upon us*, he lamented.

But then his *A Short Introduction to English Grammar* (1762) also has some nice, natural-sounding examples such as *get me some paper, get to the end of, get the better* of and *get themselves a name*. One of my early schoolteachers (not the one I thank in the acknowledgements to this book, I hasten to add) would have had him say *bring me some paper, reach the end of, defeat* and *acquire a name for themselves*. Lowth might even have been told to stand in the corner.

So, *get* or *gotten*? Use whatever you've got(ten) used to but always think about the context and situation you're speaking or writing in.

See also DUNNO, GONNA, GOTTA, WANNA

The passive with *get* (she got fired)

The passive voice in sentences such as *He was arrested for shoplifting* and *She was charged with manslaughter* can also be rendered as *He got arrested for shoplifting* and *She got charged with manslaughter*. The *get* versions are more informal and much more common in speaking than in writing.

Interestingly, corpora (large databases) of spoken English tend to show that the *get*-passive is more frequently used for bad news (people get arrested, beaten up, locked out, thrown out; things get stolen, damaged, etc.) than for good news (get elected, awarded, promoted). Maybe that says more about our lives than about grammar.

GO IN SPEECH REPORTS (HE GOES, "WHERE ARE YOU?")

Go can be used informally instead of *say* in reports of what someone said. It is often used in the historic present tense (i.e. the present tense used to dramatize past events):

*He looks at me and he **goes**, "I know you from somewhere."*

The use of *go* to report speech dates back at least to Charles Dickens' time (though he uses the past tense, *went*); it occurs in *The Pickwick Papers* (1836-7), chapter IX, reporting the shouts of post-boys on a coach. Elsewhere in *The Pickwick Papers*, Dickens uses *went* to report the noise of gunshots (chapter XIX) and the rap of a door-knocker (chapter XXXVI), so we can see why *go* emerged as an apt verb for reporting speech and sounds.

Remember that this use of *go* is extremely informal.

See also LIKE

H- IN WORDS LIKE HISTORIC AND HOTEL

I'm often asked which is better: *a historic moment* or *an historic moment*, and whether the 'h' is pronounced when people write *an historic moment*, or *an hotel*. The pronunciation *'otel* now sounds outdated, as does *'istoric*. So, you can always safely say *a historic event at a hotel near Hampstead Heath* and sound every h-, but take a deep breath before you do.

Just the other day, a historian (or should that be *an historian*?) on a BBC TV documentary referred to late Medieval England as being a society where the common people looked up to *an hereditary nobility* (with the *h-* sounded), and a commentator on BBC Radio 4 news similarly pronounced *an historic gap* with a sounded *h-*. Both came over as strangely quaint and old-fashioned, but ever so scholarly.

HAD BETTER

In informal speaking and in some dialects, the *had* is often dropped:

You better *make sure you get there on time.* (informal/non-standard)

The government **had better** *take more notice of its backbenchers.* (standard)

HARDLY and HARD

In former times, *hardly* was used to mean 'in a hard or violent way'. In Mary Shelley's *Frankenstein* (1818), we find *My pulse beat so quickly and hardly...* Nowadays it means 'only just' or 'barely/scarcely'.

I **hardly** *see my cousins at all these days except at weddings and funerals.*

Hard is used instead to refer to difficult or violent actions and events.

*She hit it so **hard** it smashed into pieces.*
*His eyesight is deteriorating. He finds it **hard** to drive at night these days.*
The thing to avoid with *hardly* in more formal contexts is slipping in a superfluous *not*:
*His voice was so quiet we **couldn't hardly** hear him.* (standard form: *we could hardly hear him*)

HAS YET TO and IS YET TO
Both these sentences are perfectly correct:
*The exact process **has** yet to be decided.*
*The exact process **is** yet to be decided.*
However, *(have) yet to* is many times more commonly used than *(be) yet to*. One or two expressions with *(be) yet to* are common enough (*is yet to be seen, is yet to come*), but the version with *have* is the preferred one in most cases.

HEADERS and TAILS (MY SON, JAMES, HE'S A PILOT)
These are the names my co-author Ronald Carter and I gave to two common phenomena in spoken English in our *Cambridge Grammar of English* (2006). Here are examples of those phenomena.
<u>Margaret, her husband, he</u>'s just got a job in Bristol, so they're moving.
<u>Her car, that new [brand name], the back of it</u> looks like a racing car.
<u>He</u>'s a very good actor, <u>Paul</u>.
Oh yes, <u>she</u>'s clever <u>is Jenny</u>.
We called the first two 'headers', since they are like headlines or like headers on an email telling you who or what the message is about. The second two are tails, because the identity of *he* and *she* are only given at the tail-end of the message. Tails are often used when giving a judgement or opinion about someone

or something. Both of these forms are very common in everyday spoken grammar and are perfectly correct, but you would probably not want to write them, especially in a formal situation.

HE/SHE, HE OR SHE, THEY (EVERY CITIZEN SHOULD DO THEIR DUTY)

This is a dilemma that presents itself particularly with words like *someone/somebody, anyone/anybody, no-one/nobody, each* and *every*.

It was all very simple in olden times because every person knew his station in life and he never complained. Examples like that last sentence and these below are now considered outdated and sexist:

*Every citizen should pay **his** taxes on time.*

*Nobody who has any self-respect would let **himself** be bullied like that.*

*Anyone who becomes aware that **he** is in possession of stolen goods should contact **his** local police force immediately.*

The debate has been over suitable replacements. Several candidates have put themselves forward and you can choose what sounds most natural, least awkward, most aligned to your politics, etc.

*If anyone doesn't have sufficient support within the party, **he or she** will be unlikely to go forward to the next round of the election.* (in speech is often heard as *he or she, he-she* or *he-stroke-she*)

*If anyone doesn't have sufficient support within the party, **he/she** will be unlikely to go forward to the next round of the election.* (in speech is often heard as *he-she, he or she,* or *he-stroke-she*)

*If anyone doesn't have sufficient support within the party, **(s)he** will be unlikely to go forward to the next round of the election.* (only applies to writing – tricky to say)

*If anyone doesn't have sufficient support within the party, **she** will be unlikely to go forward to the next round of the election.* (a way of fighting back after years of imbalance but no more gender-neutral than *he*)

*If anyone doesn't have sufficient support within the party, **they** will be unlikely to go forward to the next round of the election.* (the easiest, most neutral and current favourite).

See also SINGULAR USE OF THEY/THEM/THEIR

HYPHENS
Hyphens: Current usage
There are several places where hyphens were traditionally considered essential, but these are changing, especially in informal types of e-communication.

Hyphens: Compound adjectives before nouns (a well-known composer)
Compare:

*She's very **well known** in literary circles.* (complement of verb *to be*)

*He's a **well-known** composer of religious music.* (before a noun)

*Their car had **broken down**.* (phrasal verb)

*A **broken-down** car was blocking the road.* (before a noun)

Other examples:

*It was a **hand-written** invitation card.*

*They had some **half-baked** plan that was doomed to failure.*

Some dictionaries give compound adjectives like *handwritten, homemade, deadpan* and *backdated* as here, i.e. as one word with no hyphen and no space; others give them as hyphenated.

Hyphens: Compound nouns (lamp-post or lamp post)
There is sometimes a choice between writing compound nouns as two words with a hyphen, as two words with a space, or as one word with no space. I have come across all of the following:

hyphenated	two words	one word
lamp-post	*lamp post*	*lamppost*
book-worm	*book worm*	*bookworm*
home-page	*home page*	*homepage*
car-park	*car park*	*carpark*

Again, dictionaries vary as to how they represent such compounds and the general trend is towards losing the hyphen. Hyphenated forms of *today, tomorrow, weekend* and *email* (*to-day, to-morrow, week-end, e-mail*) now look dated.

Where hyphens are still used (sister-in-law, self-catering)

Hyphens survive in compounds like *sister-in-law* and *son-in-law*. They are also used in expressions such as *vice-president, self-catering, a ten-year-old car* and in numbers written out (*sixty-six, twenty-four*). Some prefixes are still commonly used with a hyphen (e.g. *multi-storey, ex-wife, non-refundable*).

In formal writing, if two compounds share a common headword, they can be combined using hyphens to avoid repeating the shared element:

*The movement brings together various **socially-** and **politically-** oriented philosophies.* (i.e. socially-oriented and politically-oriented)

When not to use hyphens (we need to set up the room)

Don't use hyphens with phrasal verbs. Phrasal verbs are verbs that have two parts, a verb and an adverb particle (e.g. *take off, set up, stand by*):

*We need to **set up** the room for the meeting.*

*BA flights usually **take off** from Terminal 5.*

***Stand by** for some exciting news.*

When the noun forms of phrasal verbs are used, single words or hyphenated forms may occur:

They put me on **standby** for the earliest flight the next day.
He did a brilliant **take-off** of Donald Trump.
See also Prefixes and hyphens

IF: THINGS TO LOOK OUT FOR
Standard form (if I won the lottery …)
Two common patterns of usage with *if* that often cause doubts, especially in more formal contexts, are the following:
If I **move** into town, I'**ll** sell my car. (simple present tense verb in the *if*-clause + *shall/will* in the main clause)
If I **won** the lottery, I **would** give up my job. (simple past tense verb in the *if*-clause + *would* in the main clause)
This is the conventional, standard pattern. However, people sometimes use an extra *would* in the *if*-clause, which is unnecessary.
If we'**d** win the lottery, we'**d** never have to work again. (non-standard)

Unnecessary additions (if it hadn't have been for him, …)
Unnecessary words seem to find their way into *if*-clauses like a virus. This is especially so when *if* is used to look back on past events.
If I **would have** known she was going to stay the night, I would have made up the spare bed. (non-standard)
If I **had** known she was going to stay the night, I would have made up the spare bed. (standard)
The sentence only needs one *would*, not two. In conversation, probably nobody will notice if you bung in the extra *would* but in formal writing, you may want to think along more traditional lines.
Some people aren't content with one form of the verb *have* and slip in an extra one. You will often hear sentences like:
If I **had have** known then what I know now, I would have trained to

be a plumber. That's where the money is. (non-standard)
*If it **hadn't have** been for him, I wouldn't have survived.*

If I had known (or, more informally, *If I'd known*) and *If it hadn't been* are all you need in these examples.

It's not only with *if* that the extra *have* is inserted. Conditional sentences without *if* attract it too. The unsuccessful Democratic Party candidate in the 2016 US Presidential election campaign, Bernie Sanders, expressed his regret in a BBC radio interview that he would not be the official nominee, by saying:

*I would **have** loved to **have** had the opportunity ...*

The unnecessary extra *have* could be taken out in two ways:

*I **would love** to **have had** the opportunity ...*
*I **would have** loved to **have** the opportunity ...*

IT'S or ITS

Here's something that screams 'bad grammar!' but which you'll find now and again even in quite formal writing:

*The team has lost **it's** way.*

Standard form: *The team has lost **its** way.*

Lots of people get in a twist about this. The reason for the confusion is that *it's* looks a bit like *Clare's* as in *Clare's car*, where the 's indicates possession.

Don't think that way. *It's* is a short form of *it is* and is like *I'm, she's, he'd* and *they'll*.

***It's** past midnight.*

Its is just a pronoun ending in -*s*, like *his*. And while we're about it, remember that *yours, hers, ours and theirs* don't have an apostrophe:

*Are these gloves **yours** or **hers**?*

See also YOU'RE and YOUR

KIND, SORT and TYPE

With these three nouns in the plural, people are often unsure

whether it is correct to say:
*There are **different kinds/sorts/types of headphone**: in-ear, on-ear and over-ear are the main ones.*
or:
*There **are different kinds/sorts/types of headphones**: in-ear, on-ear and over-ear are the main ones.*
The second version (two plurals) was traditionally considered the correct one, but both forms are perfectly acceptable.
People are often uncertain as to the use of the singular form. Subtle differences of meaning are possible between singular and plural:
*What **type of dog** is your favourite?* (I'm thinking you'll choose one type)
*What **kinds of films** do you prefer?* (there may be several: thrillers, comedies, etc.)
*What **sort of music** do you think we should have at your party?* (we need to choose one sort)
*What **sorts of music** do you like?* (there may be several: rock, classical, jazz)
As always, be prepared to see all sorts of combination(s) of these 'rules'.

LESS and FEWER

This is one that purists get vexed about. The conventional rule is that *less* is for nouns we normally do not use in the plural. These are mass or uncountable nouns such as *equipment, flour, furniture, information, petrol, progress, rice.*
*Our new car uses a lot **less petrol** than the old one.*
*Those cupcakes turned out okay but I think I'll use a bit **less sugar** next time.*
Fewer is for nouns in the plural.
*You see **fewer** and **fewer birds** on farmland these days. It's worrying.*

Fewer people are wearing watches; they just use their phones to tell the time.

However, this is a rule that is observed more in the breach than the observance, and everywhere you're likely to hear and see *less people, less times, less emails* - in fact less of just about everything. Supermarket express checkouts have been known to change their signs from *Five items or less* to *Five items or fewer*, probably after protests from purists, but only the grammarian's equivalent of King Cnut would try to turn back the tide on this one.

LET'S

It's easy to forget the apostrophe when shortening *let us*:
Let's *stop now. I've had enough.*
Most spell-checkers are good at picking that up.
Without the apostrophe, *lets* can be a present-tense verb or a plural noun:
*He **lets** me borrow his bike when he's not using it.*
*Most of the cottages along the coast are holiday **lets**.* (properties to rent)

LIE or LAY

Take a deep breath. This is an easy one to jumble up, then you learn the correct way, then you forget it again.

Lie, lay lain

Lie is an irregular verb, i.e. its various parts don't follow the normal rule of adding *-ed* to make the past tense and past participle. Its different parts are *lie* (present), *lying* (present participle), *lay* (past), *lain* (past participle). It doesn't take an object.
*When we go on holiday, we just **lie** on the beach all day.*
*Nicola **was lying** on the sofa, watching TV, when suddenly a thought struck her.*
*Yesterday I just **lay** in bed all day feeling wretched.*

*He'd **lain** unattended in a hospital corridor for six hours before help arrived.*

Lay, laid, laid

Lay has these parts: *lay* (present), *laying* (present participle), *laid* (past), *laid* (past participle). It takes an object (underlined).

Lay <u>*your money*</u> *on the table first. Then I'll deal the cards.*

*Our hens were **laying*** <u>*about half a dozen eggs*</u> *every day. We ended up giving eggs to all the neighbours.*

*The talks **laid*** <u>*a solid foundation*</u> *for the subsequent peace-treaty.*

*The retreating army had **laid*** <u>*roadside mines*</u>.

The trouble is, people often say things like this:

If you're not feeling well, go and lay down for an hour.

I'm looking forward to not working and just laying on the beach for two weeks.

And nobody bats an eyelid. Especially when they're lying on the beach with their eyes closed.

However, if you say *She just lied on the beach all day*, you're suggesting someone spent a whole day telling untruths and you may end up being sued for lie-bel.

LIKE (IT WAS CRAZY, LIKE!)

People often complain that careless and lazy speakers (titles usually aimed at teenagers and other younger people) can't say a sentence without every other word being *like*, including for introducing speech reports:

*So, **like** he just like comes in and he's **like**, "Who the hell are you?" and I'm **like**, "Well, who the hell are* <u>*you*</u>*?" **Like** it was crazy **like**!*

These uses of *like* in informal speech are a badge of identity among friends and intimates. They do no harm to anyone and are used by all age groups. The use of *like* as in *It was crazy like* is hundreds of years old, but, as with any non-standard or highly informal grammar, there is a time and place for it and it may

project entirely the wrong or undesired image of a person if used in inappropriate situations.
See also GO IN SPEECH REPORTS

LIKELY

This is one of several grammatical grey squirrels; the American English version is becoming more and more common in British usage. This was the traditional distinction:
*The election **is likely to** take place early next year.* (British)
*The election **will likely** take place early next year.* (American)
In other words, British English treats *likely* as an adjective (compare *is certain to take place*). American English treats it as an adverb (compare *will certainly take place*). Both ways of using the word are venerably ancient.

LOAN WORDS (KEBAB, MACHO)

English has been borrowing from other languages since time immemorial. It has an open and easy-going attitude to borrowing: if a loan word fits the bill and is felt to be usable to describe some new phenomenon, then in it comes. The only issue may be whether we anglicise loan words in grammar and/or pronunciation.

French accounts for a huge number of borrowings, from *café* to *déjà-vu* (but you may have already sensed I was going to say that one). Overseas imperial adventures, trade and other types of contact between languages account for many other words such as *pyjamas* (Persian and Urdu), *catamaran* (Tamil), *cha* (tea: Cantonese), *alcohol* (Arabic). Music has brought us from Italian *alto, largo, soprano* and many other terms. Food is an ever-growing domain of loan words as the British become more adventurous in culinary experiences: *pizza* (Italian), *smorgasbord* (Swedish), *sushi* (Japan), *taco* (Mexican Spanish) are just a few that have entered the language in the last century.

Shakespeare loved including foreign words in his plays, often, as Norman Blake puts it in his book on Shakespeare's use of non-standard English forms, *to emphasize the pomposity of the speaker* (p.120). Foreign words in Shakespeare often come from Spanish and Italian.

Pronunciation and grammar are often anglicised over time, so we say *pizzas*, not *pizze* and we talk about the *altos* and *sopranos* in a choir; these plurals would not be correct in Italian. Recently, the importation of the Spanish word *machismo* (used to describe an exaggerated and sexist male behaviour) has caused some to anglicise the pronunciation to *mackismo*, while others retain the Spanish pronunciation, where the *-ch-* is as in *church*.

And it took me years to learn how to spell *yogurt* (*yoghurt*?).

MADE OF, FROM, WITH, OUT OF

Made of usually describes the basic substance or material that composes something: *a brooch made of pure gold, a worktop made of stainless steel.*

Made from tends to be used for things created by re-using material in some way or mixing materials: *a compost bin made from recycled plastic, whisky made from a blend of grains.*

Made with is useful for talking about ingredients, especially in food preparation: *pasta made with organic flour and free-range eggs, a dish made with butternut squash and coconut milk.*

Made out of usually describes a process of changing the function of something: *a picnic table made out of an old beer-crate, a doggie poop-scoop made out of an empty milk carton.*

Oh, that it were that simple! Be prepared to hear any one of these forms used for any one of the meanings. What I've given here are the traditional differences.

MALAPROPISMS (ACRIMONIAL DEBATES)

Getting words not quite right can produce hilarious results. I recall almost falling out of bed with laughter a few years ago, when waking up to a morning radio news programme and hearing someone venting his rage about allegations of fraud that had been made concerning trade-union elections. The interviewee said the allegations were serious and that the *alligators* should produce their evidence. *Allegator* and *alleger* existed centuries ago as noun forms of the verb *to allege* but have fallen out of usage, so we can forgive the speaker – the English lexicon failed him in his hour of need. Someone should invent a good, serviceable noun for 'one who alleges' and make it snappy.

Shakespeare used malapropisms to great satirical and humorous effect. The character Bottom in *A Midsummer Night's Dream* (Act III, scene 1) refers to *the flowers of odious savours sweet* (odorous). Norman Blake's book on the Bard's use of non-standard forms lists numerous examples of purposefully exploited malapropisms. Just recently, on a TV news programme, the newscaster (presumably reading off an autocue) quoted a public figure as having said that the return of grammar schools in England would be *socially diversive* (divisive).

Also recently, an academic, commenting in a BBC TV documentary on the amount of misogyny on the internet, said: *People feel they can say what they want with importunity* (impunity).

Others I have come across over the years include *emergency heater* (immersion heater), *lesbian restaurant* (Lebanese restaurant), *bisexual hairdresser's* (unisex hairdresser's), *furniture with tubercular legs* (tubular legs), *youngsters from depraved backgrounds* (deprived), *aquifiers* (aquifers), *acrimonial debates* (acrimonious), *obeast* (obese) and a *misspelt youth* (*misspent*).

Most famous of all are some of ex-US President George W. Bush's efforts, my personal favourite being his assertion that *they*

misunderestimated the Commander in Chief.
Tip: when in doubt, insult a good dictionary.

MAY BE and MAYBE
May be as two words is a modal verb plus the main verb *be*. Modal verbs are verbs like *can, could, must, might, would* and so on. They express degrees of possibility or desirability.
*It **may be** a good idea to have your passport with you at the bank. They **might** ask you for some ID.*
Maybe written as one word is an adverb meaning that something is possible or could be true. It's an informal version of *perhaps*.
*He's late. **Maybe** there's been a problem on the motorway or something, or **perhaps** he's just forgotten.*

MEDIA
Media is the plural of *medium*, but it is often used as a singular noun referring to radio, TV and the press, or social media, as a collective idea.
*The fax as a **medium** of communication is now virtually obsolete.* (singular noun)
*News is now available in a variety of different **media**, not just through the press and broadcasting.* (plural noun)
*The **media** needs to be constantly on guard against state intervention.* (singular noun: radio, TV and the press)
*Social **media** often drives the news agenda these days.* (the various online sharing media)

METER and METRE
A *meter* is an automatic measuring instrument, as in *gas meter, speedometer, thermometer.*
A *metre* is the standard measurement of length in the metric system, as in *100 metres, five kilometres, eight centimetres.*

As always, there's a complication: American English uses the spelling *millimeter, centimeter, meter, kilometer*. I've had to stop my spell-checker from automatically changing them to the British spelling in order to show them here.

Some people say *KILometres*, others say *kiLOmetres*. Both pronunciations are in widespread usage.

MISPLACED PARTICIPLES (A HARE DRIVING HOME)

A lot of fuss is made about these and they are often the source of humour, but people usually understand what the intended meaning is in context. Here's an example. The participle clause (or *-ing* clause) is underlined:

I saw a hare <u>driving home from Cambridge the other day</u>. (maybe the hare had popped in to use the excellent university library)

It's just one to watch out for. There are easy solutions to make things unambiguous, such as moving the participle clause around and/or making the subject explicit:

When I was driving home from Cambridge the other day, I saw a hare.

MISS

No, this is not about *Ms, Miss and Mrs*. They're in the next entry. This is a funny one you hear quite a lot:

*Since we moved into a flat, we **miss not** having a garden.*

What they miss is *<u>having</u> a garden*. The *not* is superfluous. But people usually understand one another in context.

MISS, MS, MRS, MR, MASTER

Miss is definitely dropping out of usage nowadays, but one should respect the choice of any woman who prefers to be addressed as *Miss*, as opposed to the rather more neutral *Ms*, which doesn't give away any marital secrets.

Mrs is hanging on longer, but, again, it is a matter of choice and that choice should be in the hands of the person addressed. We shouldn't be dismissive of, or sneer at, people's choices in such matters.

What is on the way out (or at least ought to be) is the following:

Mr and Mrs John Wilson *invite George Lewoski to the wedding of their daughter, Grace, to Manfred Gries.*

Presumably, wife and husband are not both called *John*.

Mr is still with us, but in recent years I've noticed how complete strangers from businesses I deal with treat me like a long-lost old pal and address me in emails as *Dear Michael*. My wife gets the same with her first name. I think we just have to live with that one. If you complain, they usually send you an apology, address you as *Mr* or *Ms* and then spell your surname wrong.

When I was a little kid in the 1950s, I used to get birthday cards from aunts and uncles addressed to *Master Michael McCarthy*. You can still do it for a laugh if you like.

NEVERTHELESS and NONETHELESS

These both mean 'despite what has gone before' or 'however'. *Nevertheless* is by far the more frequent in both speaking and in writing, and both words are less frequent in speaking than in writing.

Nonetheless can also be written as three separate words (*none the less*), but writing it as one word is twice as common.

NOUNS, VERBS, ADJECTIVES: TYPES OF WORDS

The table shows the main word-classes that you should know about in order to understand grammar more effectively.

name	explanation	example(s)
noun	name of a person, place, idea or thing	book, engineer, Zoe, Marcus, London, friend, life, music
countable noun	noun that can be made plural	pen(s), tree(s), boy(s)
mass or uncountable noun	noun not normally used in the plural	information, rice, furniture, progress, petrol
verb	word expressing a state, action or process	sing, grow, seem, be, have, will, can, allow, write
adjective	word describing a quality possessed by a noun	big, lovely, disturbing, amazing, laughable, wooden, Polish
adverb	word that says something about an action, process or quality	quickly, often, sadly, alright, immediately
preposition	word that shows a relationship (e.g. time, place) between words or phrases	in, at, on, of between, from
pronoun	words that refer to people and things without using a full noun	me, she, it, ours, I, him, those, someone, nobody, we, you, who

OFF

Off is a preposition or an adverb.

They jumped **off** the bridge and swam in the river. (preposition)

When I went to open the shed door, the handle fell **off**. (adverb)

In some dialects people say *of* after *off*. This is often heard in American English.

*It was a belt with something like a purse hanging **off of** it.*

*Adam said we should stay **off of** the floor for a few hours while the varnish dries.*

In standard English, *off* doesn't need *of* after it; it's already a preposition.

OLDER, ELDER, OLDEST and ELDEST

Both the *o*-forms and the *e*-forms can refer to comparisons of two people's age, but *older* and *oldest* are by far the more frequent and are used to refer to people and things. *Elder* is normally used about family relations and is most typically used before a noun, except in expressions such as *the elder of the two / the elder of whom.*

*Who's **older**, you or your sister?* (Not *Who's elder?*)

*There were two brothers, the **elder** of whom, Archie, was killed in the war.*

*When the parents got divorced, her **elder/older** brother went to live with their father.*

The eldest is often used without anything following:

*They had three children: Rita, Fran and Kenneth. Rita was the **eldest**.* (or *Rita was the oldest*)

For places and things, *older* and *oldest* are used:

*We've always wanted to live in an **older** house, not one of these modern boxes with no garden.*

*St Andrews is the **oldest** university in Scotland.*

ONES and ONE'S

Ones is a pronoun for referring to plural things instead of using or repeating a full noun.

*I can only see my black shoes here. Where are my brown **ones**?*

One's is a rather formal word. It's the possessive form of the pronoun *one*, which means 'me and anyone else who shares my world view'.

*One hates to see **one's** best efforts come to nothing.*

PAST and PASSED

Past is a noun, adjective or adverb.

*They just want to forget the **past** and look to the future.* (noun)
*They've learnt a lot from their **past** mistakes.* (adjective)
*I was crossing the road when a police car drove **past** at high speed.* (adverb)

Passed is the past tense of the verb *to pass* (yes, I know; I just can't think of a better way of expressing it).

*We **passed** by your house yesterday but your car wasn't there so we assumed you were out.* (compare *We drove past your house ...*)
*She **passed** him a piece of paper with an email address written on it.*

PAST TENSE (TOOK) and PAST PARTICIPLE (TAKEN)
Forms and examples

English verbs are often listed in terms of their several parts, typically the three main ones of base-form, past tense and past participle. Examples:

base form	past tense	past participle
live	lived	lived
arrive	arrive	arrived
take	took	taken
fall	fell	fallen
see	saw	seen
sit	sat	sat
put	put	put

Live and *arrive* are *regular* verbs: they just add *-ed* for past tense and past participle. The others are irregular, sometimes with a shared irregular past and past participle (e.g. *sat*), sometimes with two different forms (e.g. *took, taken, fell, fallen*), while for *put*, all three parts are the same.

The past participle is used with *have* (for present and past perfect) and *be* or *get* (for the passive voice):

*We've **lived** here for 30 years.* (present perfect)

*Margaret had **fallen** asleep on the sofa and didn't hear the doorbell.* (past perfect)

*She was/got **charged** under the Prevention of Terrorism Act.* (passive voice)

In some regional dialects, an irregular past tense is used as the past participle:

*I haven't **took** the dog for a walk yet; I'll clean the floor when I get back.* (standard form: *taken*)

*We've never **wrote** a letter complaining about anything before now, have we?* (standard form: *written*)

In 1751, the grammarian James Harris in his grammar, *Hermes*, refers to *a corruption, at present so prevalent* of using the past instead of the past participle in utterances such as *it was wrote* and *he was drove*. So, what's new?

Vice-versa, in some dialects, an irregular past participle is sometimes used as the past tense.

*I **seen** him yesterday.* (standard: *saw*)

*Ronnie **done** that; don't blame me!* (standard: *did*)

*I **drunk** too much last night.* (standard: *drank*)

If you speak a dialect that uses such forms, don't be ashamed or feel you have to change. No dialect is inherently better than any other. The British Royal Family and posh politicians all use dialects; it's just that they use the established, so-called educated, powerful dialects of the upper-middle and upper classes which we no longer think of as dialects. The important thing is to be aware of dialect features and to use them in appropriate circumstances and to orientate towards the established standard when you feel it's more appropriate.

Past tense and past participle ending in -t or -ed (learnt or learned)
Some verbs have two possible past tenses, one ending in -t, the other in -ed. Common ones are *burn* (*burnt* or *burned*), *dream* (*dreamt* or *dreamed*), *learn* (*learnt* or *learned*), *leap* (*leapt* or *leaped*) and *spell* (*spelt* or *spelled*).
*They've **spelt/spelled** my name wrong on this list.*
*By the age of 30, she had **learnt/learned** three foreign languages to a decent level of fluency.*
*I **burnt/burned** my finger on the frying pan.*
Both endings are common in British English, while the -ed endings are preferred in American English.

PHRASES, CLAUSES, SENTENCES

term	explanation	example(s)
phrase	group of words acting together as a unit	*in the kitchen, the blue car, quite nice, very slowly*
clause	group of phrases including a verb (underlined)	*she laughed, I love pears, to get there early, if you're unhappy, while cycling home the other day*
main clause	clause that can stand on its own	*It rained, We all applauded, Get real! Cats drink milk.*
subordinate clause	clause that needs to be attached to a main clause to make full sense	*when I got home, because it's unfair, if you're rich, to solve the problem, sailing down the river*
sentence	clause or group of clauses, of which at least one must be a main clause (underlined)	*When you're ready, we can start.* *She sang and he played the guitar. We all cried.* *I listen to the radio while driving.*

PREFIXES (UN-, IN-, DIS-)
Prefixes: Use and examples
Prefixes are added to the beginning of words to change the meaning in various ways, for example to create the opposite meaning (*unreal, impossible*) or to indicate a time (*preschool, midweek*). They don't normally have hyphens, with some exceptions (see Prefixes and hyphens). Some examples with adjectives and their opposites:

adjective	prefixed adjective
possible, polite	*impossible, impolite*
legible, legal, logical	*illegible, illegal, illogical*
regular, responsible	*irregular, irresponsible*
respectful, loyal	*disrespectful, disloyal*
able, known, suitable	*unable, unknown*
capable, active	*incapable, inactive*

Although there are patterns here, they're not always an infallible guide: *plausible* becomes *implausible*, but *pleasant* becomes *unpleasant*. *Invaluable* is not the opposite of *valuable*. Use a good dictionary if in doubt.

Prefixes: Variant forms (unfeasible, infeasible)
Sometimes, there are variants: both *unfeasible* and *infeasible* are found as opposites of *feasible*; *unfeasible* is the more frequently used. You can *unfriend* or *defriend* someone on social media; *unfriend* seems to have won that battle. *Untransferable* exists, but *non-transferable* is half a dozen times more common. *Non-negotiable* is many times more used than its neglected but equally correct sidekick, *unnegotiable*. Someone used *untransparent* on the radio recently, but *non-transparent* is far more frequent.

Then there are historical fights for dominance. *Unelegant* is attested as the opposite of *elegant* in the 16th century but seems to have been overtaken by *inelegant* by the end of the 18th century. Another example is *untractable* (in use from the 16th century till the first part of the 19th), overtaken since then by *intractable*. Similarly, *unpolite* and *impolite* co-existed for a long while; *impolite* emerged as 'king of the castle' by the mid-18th century.

When I was a kid, any material or substance that caught fire easily was called *inflammable*. By some obscure decree of the powers that be, this lost its prefix and became *flammable*. But not so fast with the indignation: *flammable* was in use 100 years ago, so it's not exactly the new kid on the block.

In 2016, media commentators just couldn't seem to agree on whether there were moves to *unendorse, de-endorse* or *disendorse* Donald Trump as a US Presidential candidate. All three popped up in one place or another.

As with all other aspects of the language, prefixes change over time.

Prefixes and hyphens (pre-1980, prewar)

Prefixes are sometimes used with hyphens, but not always. These are some prefixes that can vary as to whether they attract hyphens:

hyphen	no hyphen
anti-war	*antimatter*
post-medieval	*postnatal*
pre-1980	*prewar*
sub-standard	*subsurface*
non-flammable	*nonnative*
mid-century	*midsummer*

Prefixed adjectives: No non-prefixed equivalents (disgruntled)

You can be *disgruntled* but not *gruntled*, though P. G. Wodehouse wrote humorously of one of his characters: "... if not actually disgruntled, he was far from being gruntled." You can be *implacable* but *placable*, though it exists, is extremely rare (my spell-checker is blowing a gasket over it). If you're *dishevelled* and tidy yourself up, are you *shevelled*? [please, spell-checker, stop changing that to *shovelled*] *Shevelled* seems to have had a short and relatively undistinguished career then faded into oblivion. It actually wasn't the opposite of *dishevelled* but meant the same as *dishevelled* with the *di-* dropped, a case of aphaeresis. Now that sounds painful.

See also CREATIVE WORD-FORMATION

PREPOSITIONS (TO, FROM, OF)
Prepositions and object pronouns (to me, from us)
Prepositions are words like *to, of, at, between, over, through, behind, on, in*. It's worth remembering that they are followed by the object form of pronouns: *me, him, her, them, us. It* and *you* have the same form for the subject and object.

A common problem that arises is when the object of the preposition is a mixed one, as in this example:

*Someone said there was a great **photo of Jamie and I** on Twitter today.*

This should be *Jamie and me*, since both individuals are governed by the preposition *of*. Lurking here may also be subconscious memories of schooldays and being told that overuse of *me* was impolite.

See also SUBJECTS and OBJECTS, BETWEEN YOU AND ME

Prepositions: Ending sentences with
Fowler in his *A Dictionary of Modern English Usage* (1926) on more than one occasion dismisses as a "superstition" the idea that prepositions should not be used at the end of a sentence. But the hoary old myth persists to a surprising extent. Dig a deep

hole and bury it. It all comes from well-meaning grammarians who thought English should be subject to the same rules as Latin, since Latin was the language of classical thought and culture and it didn't allow so-called 'stranded' prepositions. The following are all happy sentences and are perfectly correct.

*I can't find any knives or forks. What are we expected to eat **with**?*
*There are all sorts of irrational things that rational people are afraid **of**.*
*Which box shall I put these books **in**?*

James Greenwood's *The Royal English Grammar* (1737), dedicated to the then HRH The Princess of Wales, cited sentences such as *Whom do you give that to?* and *He is the person I gave it to* as examples of the preposition being *put out of its natural place* but seemed to accept it as in common use. Another 18th-century grammarian who fretted about where prepositions ought to be placed and ought not to was the Lord Bishop of Oxford, Robert Lowth. He wanted prepositions to be used in ways that suited *the solemn and elevated style* but admitted that stranded prepositions prevailed in conversation. (His *Short Introduction to English Grammar* was published in 1762. The 1799 edition cost three shillings in old money.)

PRINCIPAL and PRINCIPLE

Principal as an adjective means 'main or most important'.
*Her **principal** source of income is writing educational textbooks.*
As a noun, it means the head of a school or college.
*The **Principal**, Mr Robert Townsend, welcomed parents to the open day.*
Principle is a noun; it means a basic idea or rule, or a moral standard or set of moral standards.
*I agree with the plan in **principle**, but we need to discuss a lot more of the details before we go ahead.*

*It is against his **principles** to avoid paying tax, even though it may not be illegal.*

PRONOUNS (I, ME, WE, US, THEY, THEM)
Subject and object pronouns (I, we, me, us)
Subject pronouns are words like *I, he, she, we, they*.
Object pronouns are words like *me, him, her, us, them*.
Here's a formally correct sentence:
***Simon and I** are going away next week.*
And here's one that a lot of people would be happy to say but which is non-standard:
***Simon and me** are going away next week.*
The two people going away form the subject of the verb, so the subject form *I* is considered correct, not the object form *me*. If Simon was not going away with you, you would just say *I'm going away next week*.

Using *me* as the subject often happens when it comes before another subject, especially in informal conversation.
***Me and my cousin** were born on the same day.*
I and my cousin would sound way too ponderous. *My cousin and I* would be okay.

But don't worry – lots of things in informal conversation pass by entirely unnoticed. Just watch out in more formal situations.

Object pronouns (let Margaret and me know)
Here's a sentence (disguised) from a business email I received recently.
*Do **let Margaret and I know** how you wish to proceed.*
Standard form: *Do let Margaret and me know how you wish to proceed.*
If Margaret wasn't involved, you wouldn't say *Do let I know how you wish to proceed*. You'd say *Do let me know*. *Me* is the object of *let*.

The same applies if you add Margaret to the sentence. You and Margaret together form the object, so you need an object pronoun.

Object pronouns (it was me/him/etc. that did it)

After *it + be* in sentences with a *who*- or *that*-clause, we use the object pronouns except in very formal situations.

*Get in touch with Mick Tyman; **it was him that** did all the plumbing.*
***It was me that** was waving to you from the bus the other day.*

Using the subject pronouns sounds very formal.

***It is I who** should apologise, and I do that now, most sincerely.*
*Please address your comments to Mr Finn. **It was he who** organised the event.*

A way around this is to say: *I am the one who should apologise / He is the one who organized ...*

Pronouns: Object and possessive forms before -ing (do you mind me asking?)

In very formal styles, sentences like the following have the possessive form (*my, your, our*, etc.) of the personal pronouns:

*Would you have any objection to **my** paying him a visit in hospital?*
*They told me about **your** needing to consult a lawyer.*

In less formal contexts it is perfectly acceptable to use the object forms of the pronouns:

*Would you have any objection to **me** paying him a visit in hospital?*
*They told me about **you** needing to consult a lawyer.*

PRONOUNS ENDING IN -ONE AND -BODY (ANYONE, SOMEBODY)

The following alternatives are equally valid:
someone/somebody
anyone/anybody
no-one/nobody
everyone/everybody

The main difference is that the forms ending in -*body* are more common in speech. The forms ending in -*one* have a slightly more formal feel and are more frequent in writing.

A query spotted recently on the internet read: *Is it better to be a real nobody than a fake somebody?* When used as full nouns in this way, meaning a person no-one has heard of (*a nobody*) and its opposite, a celebrity of some sort (*a somebody*), the -*body* ending is always used.

PROVIDED and PROVIDING (THAT)

Both forms are standard and both are more common in writing than in speaking. *That* is often omitted:

*You can build without planning permission, **provided (that)** the extension does not exceed a certain percentage of the existing building.*

***Providing** you're prepared to put in the time, being on the committee can be very rewarding.*

As long as and *so long as* can be used with the same meaning and sound slightly less formal.

See also: AS LONG AS and SO LONG AS

QUESTION MARK

Direct questions (is she your teacher?)

Question marks (?) are used at the end of sentences with what linguists call interrogative clauses. Interrogative clauses involve words like *do, did, have, had, can, must, should, will, is, are, was*, etc., followed by a subject and a main verb. They are used to ask direct questions.

Are you coming with us?
Did she get that job she was after?
Why do people complain so much?
Wouldn't most of us prefer a later start? What do you think?

Since you're here, could you help us put out some tables and chairs?
The same applies after question tags (*are they? will she? don't we?* etc.).
*We've been lucky with the weather lately, **haven't we**?*
*The boss likes her coffee black, **does she**?*
The verb *to be* (and sometimes, more formally, *to have*) can themselves be used as main verbs in interrogative clauses.
***Are you** an engineer, by any chance?*
***Has she** any particular dietary requirement we should be aware of?*
See also EXCLAMATION MARK

Statements heard as questions (you're not coming with us then?)
People very often also use a question mark at the end of a statement which they want to be heard as a question. Purists will probably frown at it, but it's not a big issue and it can be quite useful in informal communications such as personal emails.
So you won't be with us next week if you're going away?
I could email her right away if you like?

Indirect questions: No question mark (I asked her if she was okay.)
You don't need a question mark after an indirect question. Indirect questions are when someone reports the asking of a question. They are typically introduced by verbs such as *ask, demand, wonder* and *enquire*.
Direct question: *Can we change our room?*
Indirect question: *We asked if / enquired whether we could change our room.*
Direct question: *Have you had time to look at that document I sent you?*
Indirect question: *I was wondering if you've had time to look at that document I sent you.*
As usual, don't be surprised if you do see question marks used

in indirect questions. People get up to all sorts of things. Just remember that, in more formal situations, more traditional conventions may give a better impression.

Question marks in polite requests (would you pass me that book?)

We often use a question mark when making polite requests, even though, strictly speaking, they are not questions (in the sense of requiring a *yes* or *no* answer):

Could you let me know which days you would be available for a meeting next week?

However, we can sometimes avoid this dilemma by using a sentence with *if…*

If you could let me know which days you would be available for a meeting next week, that would be most helpful.

Rhetorical questions

Rhetorical questions are questions that don't demand an answer from the reader or listener, and the questioner probably already has an answer in mind. They are often used just to raise a topic in the reader's or listener's mind. They end with a question mark.

The draft bill proposes changes to the regulations on food labelling. ***Why are the government doing this?*** *It could be consumer pressure or there might be more sinister reasons.*

QUOTATION MARKS / INVERTED COMMAS ("…")

It is customary to mark direct speech in some way, most typically by using either single or double inverted commas, often informally referred to as 66-99 (" …"). The reporting verb (*say, ask, tell, reply, shout*, etc.) is separated from the words spoken by a comma, which comes before the quotation mark. Final punctuation, such as a full stop, exclamation mark or question mark, comes before the closing quotation mark

He asked, "What should we do now?"

"Leave town immediately," she replied.

Here I've used double quotation marks, but single ones do just as well.

'What a dreadful mess!' she said as she walked into the room.

A random (i.e. totally unscientific) sample of novels on my bookshelf shows a definite preference for single quotation marks, so a lot of printer's ink has been saved. A similar sample of academic books shows an occasional preference for a colon to introduce quotations from scholarly works.

Short scholarly quotations and citations generally prefer the final quote mark to come before other punctuation marks:

Beirkov (1996) refers to such phenomena as "non-evidential".

See also COLON

RAISE, RISE and ARISE

This one is like LIE or LAY, or like quantum theory: you read about it, you think you've got it, then you go to bed, wake up the next morning and it's all a fuzzy again. So don't worry.

Rise

Rise has these parts: *rise* (present), *rising* (present participle), *rose* (past), *risen* (past participle). It doesn't take an object.

*Petrol prices **rise** when the oil price **rises** but they don't seem to go down when it falls.*

*Spring has arrived and the temperature **is rising**.*

*Shares **rose** on the London Stock Exchange yesterday.*

*Wages **have risen** by an average of 1.2% this year.*

Raise

Raise has these parts: *raise* (present), *raising* (present participle), *raised* (past), *raised* (past participle). It takes an object (underlined).

*I don't want to **raise** your hopes but I think there's a vacancy coming up soon in our office which would suit you.*

*They **raised** their prices during the recession. It was a mistake.*

By now you'll have guessed: there's a complication. It concerns the nouns *rise* and *raise*. We normally talk about a pay-rise or price-rise.

*I'd be afraid to ask my boss for a **pay-rise**, but some people do.*

However, on its own, *raise* is often used to mean an increase in wages or salary, especially in American English, which is probably influencing British English.

*I'm due for a **raise** next year so I'll be a bit better off.*

Arise

Arise (arising, arose, arisen) is similar to *rise* and is used for abstract contexts, where it means 'happen' or 'occur'.

*A problem has **arisen** in connection with your order. Please contact us at this telephone number.*

That's an example you'll be familiar with.

REFLEXIVE PRONOUNS (MYSELF, YOURSELF)

The singular reflexive pronouns are *myself, yourself, herself, himself, oneself* and *itself*. The plural ones are *ourselves, yourselves* and *themselves*.

We use reflexive pronouns when the subject and object are the same person or thing.

*Sometimes **I** ask **myself** what on earth I'm doing in this job.*

They *protected **themselves** against possible encounters with bears by wearing bells around their ankles.*

Reflexive pronouns can also be used for *the full emphatical expressing of the person*, as the grammarian James Greenwood put it in 1711. He cites *thou thy Self, we our Selves* and so on, written as separate words in his book (and with the capital letters as shown). This function of the reflexive is still in common use:

I myself *would never ask such a big favour of a friend.*

*I know that **you yourself** have experienced similar problems.*

But here's one you'll see and hear when people are trying to be extra polite:

*I'd like to invite Jane and **yourself** to join me for lunch at our London office.*

You and Jane will do fine, thank you. This polite use of *yourself* is by no means new. James Harris, in his 1751 grammar, *Hermes*, dedicates the book to the Lord High Chancellor, with the words:

*My Lord, As no-one has exercised the Powers of Speech with juster and more universal applause, than **yourself**; I have presumed to inscribe the following Treatise to your Lordship …* [punctuation as in the original]

It seems that people consider it correct and very polite to say things like the following, which a decidedly posh woman said on TV recently:

*My friends and **myself** moved here for that reason.* (standard form: *My friends and I*)

And here's one that you often hear which is a dialect form but which you'd probably want to avoid in writing and in more formal contexts.

*They set **theirselves** a target of competing in the 2020 Olympics.*

Occasionally, you will also hear *theirself* or *themself*. A poignant national appeal by the Samaritans a couple of decades ago reminded the reader that by the time they had read the text: *someone will have tried to kill themself*. It's clear why they put it this way, trying to avoid the plural *themselves* in order to urge the reader to focus on a real, individual person, even though it is non-standard. Here's another example, in this case suggesting a single, collective body:

*It's an issue the Green Party has claimed for **themself**; they want it to be their issue.*

The standard form is *themselves*, but be prepared to see and hear variations.

REGARD (WITH REGARD TO, AS REGARDS)
This concerns the expressions *with regard to, in regard to* and *as regards*. All three are in widespread usage, but *with regard to* is the most frequent and *in regard to* the least frequent.

*I am writing **with regard to** your recent announcement concerning vacant seats on the Parish Council.*

*A public fireworks display can be hellish expensive **as regards** insurance.*

RELATIVE CLAUSES (THE GIRL WHO BROKE THE WINDOW)
Relative clauses (clauses that specify or add information introduced by *who, whose, whom, which* and *that*) can be a headache. Be patient: there are only basically three types you need to worry about.

Defining relative clauses (a van that was left unattended)
These are clauses that give essential information about a noun. In these examples, taking away the underlined clauses leaves us with very little information about who or what is being referred to, or with something that means something different.

Any person who causes wilful damage to the property will be prosecuted.

A van that was left unattended near the airport entrance led to the area being evacuated.

A woman whose bicycle was stolen five years ago was surprised to find it parked against the wall of her house.

Defining relative clauses are not separated off by commas.

Non-defining relative clauses (Waterford, which is Ireland's oldest city, ...)
These are ones where the information in the relative clause is extra. We can leave it out without damaging the main message.

Waterford, which is Ireland's oldest city, was founded by Viking raiders.

Eric, to whom everyone looked for guidance, mounted the stage and began to speak.

Non-defining relative clauses are separated off by commas.

Sentential relative clauses or comment clauses (…, which is pretty cheap really)

These are *which*-clauses that comment on a whole clause or sentence.

It cost £28, which is pretty cheap really.

As the job got harder and harder, which it did, I began to have second thoughts.

Sentential relative clauses are separated off by commas.

Not so complicated after all.

See also WHO, WHICH, WHOM, WHOSE, THAT and WHAT

RIGHT(LY), WRONG(LY)

These are cases where the basic, everyday adverb doesn't end in *-ly*.

*They never **spell** my name **right**.*

*It all started to **go wrong** when Norman and Paula joined the committee.*

H. M. Queen Elizabeth II, in 1975, when ceremonially turning on the flow of North Sea oil to Britain, said:

*If we use it **right**, this flood of energy can, without doubt, much improve our economic wellbeing.*

Rightly and *wrongly* are mostly used before past participles and have a meaning of 'justifiably' and 'unjustifiably':

*She was **rightly annoyed** by what was said.*

*The men were **wrongly accused** of being involved in terrorist activity.*

Tight(ly) is a bit different.

***Tie** it **tight/tightly** now; otherwise it'll all fall out.* (You're likely to hear both.)

*All the sheaves are then **tightly bound** with raffia string.*

***Hold tight**, darling! We don't want you falling out of the boat.*

Hold tight! is a fixed phrase. It always sounded mildly absurd and over the top to me whenever I rode on the driverless shuttle at one of Britain's leading airports and a recorded voice advised everyone to *hold tightly!* as the shuttle was about to leave.

See also HARDLY and HARD

SEMICOLON

Back in 1995, a learned scholar published a paper that included in its title *The Rise and Fall of the Semicolon*[3]. Apparently it was all the rage in the 17th and 18th century. It seems to have set off on a downward trajectory since then.

The American satirical writer Kurt Vonnegut, in his 2005 collection of essays *A Man Without a Country*, discouraged the use of semicolons, referring to them as *representing absolutely nothing*.

If, like me, you'd be sad to see such a nice old friend disappear from the face of the earth, then here's what it's for. Use it or lose it.

A semicolon (;) separates two main clauses. It suggests a shorter pause for thought and a stronger connection between the two clauses than a full stop, but a more decisive break than using *and*.

*At 70, you can renew a UK driving licence online **and** you don't have to take a new test.*

*At 70, you can renew a UK driving licence online**;** you don't have to take a new test.*

*At 70, you can renew a UK driving licence online**.** **Y**ou don't have to take a new test.*

All three are correct. It's your choice as to how strong you want the link to be.

Some writers use the semicolon to separate items in lists, especially where there are longer items, instead of using commas. Have a

---

[3] Bruthiaux, P. (1995) The Rise and Fall of the Semicolon: English Punctuation Theory and English Teaching Practice. *Applied Linguistics* 16 (1): 1-14.

look at the list of people I've thanked in the acknowledgements at the beginning of this book, where I've used semicolons in this way. It sometimes doesn't look too good but it doesn't portend the end of civilisation as we know it either.

SHALL and WILL
In my day, we were taught that *shall* was for first person subjects *I* and *we*, and *will* was for second (*you*) and third person (*he, she, it, they*).

*I **shall** never forget the day my daughter was born.*

*They **will** arrive sometime next week; we **shall** be able to confirm the exact time in the next few days.*

However, this varies widely across British and Irish dialects, with many (including my own) preferring *will* for all persons:

*We **will** have to apply for a visa but we can do it online.*

Shall is widely used to make suggestions or proposals (e.g. the fixed formula *Shall we dance?*), though some dialects permit *will*:

Shall/Will *I get some more milk while I'm at the shop?*

As always, don't think your dialect is inferior. Just make the choice you think is most appropriate for the situation. In everyday speaking, *shall* and *will* both normally contract to 'll after a subject, so the difference is less important; it's in writing that the choice becomes more apparent.

SIGHT or SITE
People often get *sight* and *site* mixed up. *Sight* is to do with seeing, while *site* refers to locations.

*I knew the Prime Minister was supposed to be there somewhere but I didn't catch **sight** of her.*

*When we're at conferences in big cities, we don't often get a chance to get out and see the **sights**.*

*The hilltop was the **site** of a Neolithic village.*

SINGULAR USE OF THEY/THEM/THEIR

Purists object to the gender-neutral use of *they* used with words like *somebody, everyone, person*, etc., but don't worry about saying:

Everyone has their own personal problems to deal with.

Somebody has left **their** phone in the meeting room. I wonder if **they** realise?

The truth is that *they/their/them/themselves* referring to a singular entity is not some modern horror perpetrated by the linguistically lazy and the politically correct acting in cahoots. Its use is attested in the highly-respected *Oxford English Dictionary* as far back as the 15th century.

The celebrated 19th century essayists Walter Bagehot and John Ruskin used the singular *they* a good century before anyone dreamt up the notion of being linguistically PC.

At some point, people will stop firing off letters to the editor about this and we can all get on with life.

SO

Interviewees on radio and TV often use *so* to start a response to a question where the answer is not a logical conclusion to or a result of the question:

Interviewer: How do you propose to express your opposition to the new runway?

Interviewee: **So,** *what we intend to do is to commission our own report...*

There's nothing wrong with this and the respondent might equally have begun the answer with *Well*. It may just be a tactic for getting a bit more thinking time.

So is by no means always related to logical conclusions or results. It is often used to launch a conversation or a new topic:

So, *how's life, Sonia?*

SOME TIME or SOMETIME

Some time (two words) means a period of time.

*It would be nice to spend **some time** together. When are you free?*

Sometime (one word) means a time that is not specified.

*We'll probably go to Florida **sometime** in the autumn when it's getting cold here.*

Sometime is also used when referring to a position or job held by someone in the past but no longer.

*George Wadden, **sometime** theatre critic and radio celebrity, has decided to become an environmental campaigner.*

Impress your friends by saying *erstwhile theatre critic* instead of *sometime* in this last example.

SPLIT INFINITIVES

I wondered whether to even waste space on this one.

Feel free to always split infinitives unless the inserted matter is so lengthy that **to**, at that point and without proper regard for your reader, a phenomenon often referred to as a lack of 'audience design', **break** up the sentence would make it impossibly difficult to read.

SUBJECTS and OBJECTS

It's useful to know the difference between subjects and objects because it affects choices like whether you say *I, she, he, we, they* or *me, her, him, them*.

The subject

The subject is the person or thing that does an action or process, or experiences a state. Subjects are underlined.

<u>She</u> *wants to change her job.*

<u>He</u>*'s happy enough.*

<u>The village hall</u> *was packed.*

<u>Two vehicles</u> *were damaged by a falling tree but* <u>no-one</u> *was injured.*

The guy who lives next door to us is Latvian.
Does your friend from Edinburgh want to stay overnight?

The object

The object is the person or thing that the verb acts upon. Objects are underlined here.

She wants to change her job.
He ignored me.
Did you pass your driving test in the end?
Turn that music off!
Patrick gave me some good advice that I don't think I will ever forget.

This last example has two objects, the direct object (underlined) and the indirect object (*me*: the person or thing that receives the object).

See AGREEMENT (CONCORD)

SUBJUNCTIVE (I INSIST THAT HE APOLOGISE)

This is probably something you were tortured with at school when you learnt French or Spanish (remember those awkward verb forms you had to use if you *said I want you to help me* or *I wanted him to join our club*?). You may have even been told that the subjunctive doesn't exist in English. It does. As with a taste for garlic, I didn't discover it till I entered my adult years.

In some ways, the English subjunctive is simple enough: the base form of the verb is always used (i.e. you don't need an *-s* ending on the present tense with *he, she, it* or a third-person noun and you don't need to mark the plural or past tense), as in these examples:

*I insist that **he apologise**; a bottle of wine through the post is not enough.*

*It was always considered important that **a male child be** taught hunting skills from an early age.*

*It is essential that **they not be** made to feel excluded.*

As is apparent, these forms belong to rather formal writing and are rare in anything but the most formal speech. If you want to use them in formal situations, they tend to follow expressions of obligation or desirability, i.e. verbs like *insist, demand, require,* and adjectives like *important, essential, imperative.*

If you don't want to use them, just insert *should* before *apologise* and *be* in the first two examples and before *not* in the third one above, and it works perfectly well.

Some subjunctives in English are common phrases that we hardly think of as subjunctive:

Someone should take responsibility, **whether it be** *the school or the parents.*

Any branch of the arts, **be it** *music, theatre, poetry, painting, is struggling financially nowadays.*

Another form of subjunctive involves using *were* instead of *was*:

If I **were** *you, I'd get a ticket now; they're selling fast.*

If I was you is often heard but it is considered non-standard.

If there **were** *to be an election tomorrow, the party would lose.*

Were *it to happen that she moved to a new address, she would probably have to apply all over again.*

Generally, American English uses the subjunctive more than British English. Elsewhere in this book, I have applauded the riches American English has bestowed on British English. Let's hope the predilection for the subjunctive doesn't get shipped across the Atlantic.

SUFFIXES (-FUL, -ITY)
Suffixes: Use and examples
Suffixes are added to the ends of words, typically to change their word-class and/or meaning, e.g. to change a noun into a verb or an adjective, or vice-versa. Some examples:

verb	noun	adjective
exploit	exploit**ation**	exploit**ative**
brut**alise**	brut**ality**	brut**al**
play	play**er**	play**ful**

Suffixes: -ic or -ical

Some adjectives have two forms, one in -ic, the other in -ical, with different meanings.

*It's a very **economical** car – we only need to fill up every couple of weeks.* (doesn't use a lot of energy, doesn't cost too much)

***Economic** policy seems to be decided by a series of knee-jerk reactions these days.*
(concerning the economy of the country)

*Wordsworth's **classic** poem, "I Wandered Lonely as a Cloud", is often mistakenly called "Daffodils".* (of the highest quality, by which other poems are judged)

*It was a **classic** case of the left hand not knowing what the right hand was doing.* (a typical example of something annoying or funny)

*BBC Radio 3 plays not only **classical** music but jazz, folk, all sorts of things.* (music of the long, formal tradition of past centuries)

*She's an expert in **classical** architecture.* (architecture of ancient Greece and Rome)

*The **historical** evidence of land ownership in the area shows the dominance of a handful of rich families.* (related to history, the study of the past)

*The signing of the Good Friday Agreement in Northern Ireland was a **historic** moment heralding the end of years of conflict.* (of great importance in history)

*English Heritage manages over 400 **historic** buildings, monuments and sites in England.* (of great importance in history)

Suffixes: Gendered/sexist terms (headmistress/waiter)

Until relatively recently, a lot of jobs were gender-marked with suffixes. Many now consider such usage as old-fashioned, inappropriate or sexist. In some cases, what used to be the male term is used for both sexes; in others, new versions have emerged. Here are just a few examples.

male	female	neutral
tailor	tailoress	tailor
murderer	murderess	murderer
headmaster	headmistress	headteacher
policeman	policewoman*	police officer
waiter	waitress	waiter, server
spokesman	spokeswoman	spokesperson
fireman	firewoman	firefighter
chairman	chairwoman	chair, chair person
manager	manageress	manager

*When I was a kid, we used to say *lady policeman* for this one.

Actor and *actress* are still both in use at the time of writing, but *actor* is steadily taking over for both sexes.

Air hostess now sounds terribly dated and *cabin steward, cabin attendant* or *cabin crew member* are fine for both sexes.

Dylan Thomas, in *Under Milk Wood*, got round the *fishermen* problem by referring to *fishers* but then immediately followed it with *tradesmen*. The same passage also includes *schoolteacher, policeman* and *postman*, so it's a mixed bag. But then D. T. knew a thing or two about poetic metre, and things were different in 1954.

Suffixes: Variants (individuality, individualism)

Sometimes two possible suffixes are available but with slightly different meanings or differences in style. A recent commentator on TV referred to the *fervency* of the beliefs of a religious group;

fervour also exists, with more or less the same meaning, and is by a great margin the more frequent of the two. Another example is *secularity* versus *secularism*, where the alternating suffixes express a subtle difference in meaning. *Secularity* means the state or situation of living without being guided by religious principles, while *secularism* refers more to the doctrine or ideology that life should be based on non-religious principles. I have read both recently in the press.

An *arbiter* is a person who is either considered the best judge or authority in a matter (e.g. a fashion magazine as *the arbiter of style*) and was, in the past, also a person appointed to sort out a dispute between two parties. This latter meaning has now been taken over by *arbitrator*.

BBC radio recently featured an interview with a young man who was working as a bicycle-courier delivering fast food, who enjoyed certain aspects of his work but didn't like *the precarity that it puts us under*. *Precariousness* is by far the more frequent noun form, but *precarity* is more specific, referring especially to insecure and/or exploitative working conditions and other types of personal insecurity.

Other examples of variants include *individuality* versus *individualism*, *hallucinative* versus *hallucinatory*.

In questions of variants concerning suffixes, a good dictionary will help with such choices.

Suffixes: Bits of 'tat' (preventive, preventative)

Sometimes an extra -*tat*-, -*at* or -*ate* syllable distinguishes variants in suffixed words. The online *Collins English Dictionary* gives both *preventive* and *preventative* as adjectives from *prevent*, but gives *preventive* as the main entry. On the other hand, the dictionary gives *interpretative* priority over *interpretive* in its headwords, albeit additionally giving a special computer-related meaning to *interpretive*. *Orientate* is given as a variant of *orient*, rather than vice-versa, but both are in frequent use.

Meanwhile, *to administer* is the preferred form for giving medicines, oaths and sacraments. *To administrate* can be applied to the management and application of information and business: *Nowadays, software licensing has become less complex and easier for developers to **administrate**.*

Suffixes: Overloading (hallucinatorily)

A TV historian recently referred to an ancient group of people as working *Herculeanly*. *Herculean efforts*, yes, but save us from tongue-twisters. In relation to the variants *hallucinative* versus *hallucinatory* mentioned above, there is the veritably tongue-strangling adverb form, *hallucinatorily* – not one to try to say if you are tired and emotional.

Changing suffixes (racialism/racism)

Back in the 1970s, people who disliked or looked down upon people of other races were called *racialists* and their attitude was referred to as *racialism*. The *-al* part of the suffix seems to have disappeared and nowadays we have *racists* and *racism*. This change seems to have started in the 1980s, since when the versions without *-al* have greatly increased in frequency. However, the adjective *racial* has fought the good fight and persists in phrases such as *racial hatred* and *racial prejudice*.

Then there's a case where whole suffixes have almost vanished. Thanks to George W. Bush's *War on Terror*, the British media have wholeheartedly abandoned the adjective *terrorist* (now mostly used as a noun referring to the person) and the noun *terrorism*. We now hear of *anti-terror police* (are they a special kind of police, or shouldn't all police be against terror?), *anti-terror laws, terror attacks, terror outrages,* events that are *non-terror-related* and so on. Back in 1981, the newspaper headline *Terror in Southall* referred to street riots in the London suburb involving gangs of youths. Nowadays, the same headline would immediately suggest a terrorist atrocity.

These two examples show that suffixes, as with any feature of language, can evolve and change over relatively short spans of time. The media play a major role in the process.

SUPERLATIVE (BEST, MOST FRIGHTENING)

Superlatives are used to single out a person or thing as having an outstanding quality in some way compared with other members of their class.

*The Finkel brothers are **the best** guitar duo I've ever heard.*
*What's **the most frightening** film you've ever seen?*
In the case of superlative adverbs, *the* is often omitted:
*Who reigned **(the) longest**, Elizabeth I, George III or Queen Victoria?*
See also COMPARATIVES

TAUTOLOGY (A ROUND SPHERE)

This is not, strictly speaking, a grammatical issue but is more an issue of style. However, it comes up so frequently in conversation with friends who think I must be a world expert on it (or at it) that it deserves some space here.

Tautologies occur when an idea is needlessly expressed twice; 'needlessly' is the key word. Poets, playwrights, orators, advertisers, etc. often repeat things for a wide range of effects. Tautologies typically prompt the question: what else could it be?

*A **round sphere** floating the sky* (what else could it be but round?)
*The tree was **hollow inside**.*
*It all happened around 10:00**am in the morning**.*
*That was our **end goal**.*

Fowler, in the monumental *A Dictionary of Modern English Usage* cites *time-scale* (for *time*), *behaviour pattern* (for *behaviour*) and *weather conditions* (for *weather*) as tautologies. Condemning *weather conditions* is a bit unfair as the term normally applies to the conditions brought about by the weather (icy roads, poor visibility, etc.), but you can sort of see what he is getting at. Other favourites that are often quoted are *factual information* and *totally unique*; these last two have more or less become fixed expressions that go largely unnoticed, though I did hear *completely unique* on the radio the other day – same difference.

Tip: try to avoid using pointlessly repeated tautologies.

THE and TO: PRONUNCIATION

Recently there seems to have been a shift in the pronunciation in standard English of *the* and *to* when they are followed by a word beginning with a vowel sound. Before a vowel sound, traditionally, *the* is pronounced 'thee' and *to* is pronounced in the same way as 'too':

the end (thee end), *the office* (thee office), *to Edinburgh* (too Edinburgh), *quarter to eight* (quarter too eight)

'Thee' and 'too' are called the strong forms of *the* and *to*. Now the trend is to use for everything what linguists call the weak forms ('tha' and 'ta' – pronounced like the 'a' in *ago*, what phoneticians call a schwa, the symbol for which is like an upside-down 'e' /ə/). And speakers now routinely produce a glottal stop after *the* and *to* before a vowel sound. A glottal stop is the sound that occurs in the parody of Cockney pronunciation of words like *water* (wa-er) and *daughter* (dau-er). Here are some examples I've heard lately on radio and TV from speakers whose accent otherwise conforms to the educated standard:

*It takes me an hour to get to **tha office**.*

*When we come to **tha end** of the process...*

*The time is coming up to a quarter **ta eight**.*

*People are often too afraid **ta ask**.*

These pronunciations have long existed in some dialects and

varieties of English but they are now becoming mainstream. It's up to you whether you retain the traditional pronunciation or adopt the trend. As always, choose what you feel is appropriate to the situation.

THERE IS and THERE ARE
This is one where speaking and formal writing differ greatly in what you can get away with.

There is takes a singular complement; *there are* takes a plural complement (complements are underlined).

There's <u>a problem</u> *with the washing machine.*
There are <u>three restaurants</u> *in the square by the station.*

However, *there's* with a plural complement is now heard so frequently in speaking that it has almost become standard usage, especially with expressions of number such as *lots of, a few, five, nine, loads of*:

There's <u>quite a few empty boxes</u> *in the garage. Do we need to keep them?*

In more formal situations, you may wish to stick to the traditional usage.

THERE, THERE'S, THEIR and THEIRS
Don't get these mixed up. *There* is either an adverb of place or an existential pronoun (i.e. it indicates the existence of something – it doesn't mean it goes around in a beret smoking a pipe):

Put it over **there** *on the table, please.* (adverb of place)
There's *a problem with this software.* (existential pronoun)

Their and *theirs* indicate possession by more than one person or thing.

Border terriers are great dogs. **Their** *coat is usually quite wiry.*
I asked Jo and Felix about that shopping bag I found in the hallway. They said it's not **theirs***. I wonder whose it is.*

Watch your grammar-checker if you use one; things like this can often slip through the net.

THOSE and THEM
A wonderful old dialect speaker in my village, now deceased, said to me with reference to one of her acquaintances:
*She lives in **them houses** down at the bottom of the village, you know.*
If this is a feature of your dialect, just remember that the standard form is ***those*** *houses* and choose appropriately, according to the situation.

TILL and UNTIL
As prepositions, these mean the same, but *until* is, overall, many times the more frequent. In speaking, the gap narrows considerably, with *until* winning only by a head.
An old-fashioned way of writing *till* as *'til* has now dropped out of usage.

TOO or TO
I'm constantly surprised by how often people get in a muddle with these in emails; it may be something to do with spell-checkers or it may be a genuine confusion. Anyway, just remember that the one that means 'also' is *too*. *To* is a preposition and is also used as a reduced reference to a previously mentioned verb.
*Jim said you're going **to** the folk festival. We're going **too**.*
*I think he should go to university but he doesn't want **to**.*
And the one that means an excess of something or more of it than you want is *too*.
*It's just **too** hot to do any gardening today.* (not ~~to~~)
Interestingly, before Shakespeare's time, *too* meaning an excess of something was often written as *to*. Just to complicate matters.

TURNED (A)ROUND AND ...

This is an example of where grammar meets rhetoric and style in speaking, though it's not one that you find much in writing.

*I said, "I've got some good news for you," and she just **turned round** and said, "Well I've got some bad news for you!"*

On most occasions, this doesn't mean that someone literally swivelled around physically. It's most often used to emphasise or dramatize a response by someone. Keep it for informal situations. See also GO IN SPEECH REPORTS

VAGUE EXPRESSIONS (THINGS LIKE THAT, OR WHATEVER)

Vague expressions such as *(and) things like that, and things, and bits and pieces, and that, or whatever, and stuff, and so on and so forth*, etc. (*etc.* is one too) are often thought of as sloppy or lazy uses of English. However, they are extremely common and essential to efficient communication:

*I've got to go and buy cutlery and pots and pans and light bulbs **and bits and pieces** for my new flat.*

*They all got drunk and were fooling around and shouting **and stuff**.*

The vague expressions project a shared world; they simply mean 'you know what I'm including here'. Imagine a world where the speaker has to tell you every item they're going to buy for their new flat. By the time they mention the bath mat, the fifth lampshade, the egg-timer, the picture-hooks, the bottle-opener, the tea-cosy, the scatter-cushions, the bread bin and the set of six coat hangers, you will have lost the will to live.

There are formality issues, with *etc.* being obviously far more formal than *and stuff*, but, as always, it's horses for courses and, as long as the expression is appropriate to the situation and level of formality, there is no problem.

WHILE and WHILST

These two mean the same, but *while* is ten times the winner when it comes to how frequently they are used overall in speaking and in writing. *Whilst* is ten times more common in writing than in speaking. In simple terms, *while* wins out, especially in everyday talk.

Both forms have a long history, and there was even a third form, *whiles*, now obsolete, which occurs around 70 times in Shakespeare's plays.

Many Yorkshire dialect speakers use *while* instead of standard English *till/until*. A taxi driver in Leeds told me he was working *while Thursday* then he was off on holiday.

WHO, WHOM, WHOSE, WHICH, THAT and WHAT
Who, which, that and what

Who refers to people, *which* refers to things; *that* can refer to both.

(1) **Who** *made this mess here?*

(2) *Musicians* **who/that** *make it to the top of their profession practise for hours every day.*

(3) **Which** *tablecloth do you want, the white one or the red one?*

(4) *Something* **which/that** *always irritates me is when the weather forecaster tells you how the weather has been rather than how it's going to be.*

(5) *A remark* **(which/that)** *he made the other day upset me.*

Which and *that* can be omitted in (5).

What is for situations where there's a more open set of choices.

What *fish would you like for dinner tomorrow?* (choose from a wide range of fish)

Compare this last example with *which* in (3), where the choice is restricted.

That's the traditional view. However, *what* is often used instead of

which even when choice is restricted:
***What** colour wine do you fancy, red or white?*
What is considered incorrect in (2), (4) and (5), though it is acceptable in some dialects.

Whose

Whose refers to possession.
***Whose** jacket is this?*
*It is a city **whose** long history is manifested in its rich cultural heritage.*
This last example could be expressed more formally as:
*It is a city **the long history of which** is manifested in its rich cultural heritage.*

Whom

Whom is the object form of *who*, i.e. it is used as the object of a verb or of a preposition. It is rather formal.
*She is a person **whom** I regard as one of my great role-models in life.* (*I* as subject regard *her* as object)
*She is a person **who/that** I regard as one of my great role-models in life.* (less formal)
She is a person I regard as one of my great role-models in life. (no relative pronoun - less formal)
***To whom** was the letter addressed?* (formal)
*She lived with a well-to-do aunt, **from whom** she received a regular income.* (formal)
***Who** was the letter addressed **to**?* (less formal)
The versions with *whom* are more common in formal writing and can sound out of place or old-fashioned in everyday conversation. Use them if you like, but be prepared for your friends to say *I'm not going out with you talking like that!*
See also: Apostrophe: *who's* and *whose*, Prepositions: ending sentences with

YOU'RE and YOUR

Because the pronunciation of *you're* and *your* is very similar in rapid speech, people sometimes confuse them in writing. *You're* means you are;

You're *a good friend; I can always rely on you.*

Your indicates possession:

*Is this **your** phone? It was on the table.*

See also: CONTRACTIONS

Z: THE LETTER

Since this book claims to be an A-Z guide, I thought it needed at least one entry under Z. Fortunately, the letter itself came to the rescue. In British English we call it *zed*, while American English calls it *zee*. My prediction is we'll all be calling it *zee* before too long.

ZEUGMA

And let us not conclude the book without a mention of zeugma. A typical example of this figure of speech is when one verb governs two ideas which are quite different, often with humorous intent:

He gave her his overcoat and a strange look.

BACKGROUND READING AND RESOURCES

A Dictionary of Modern English Usage.

By H. W. Fowler. 1926. Oxford: Oxford University Press.

A classic by a great observer of English usage and a book that is still quoted as an authority today, thanks to its several editions, including an updated one in 2015. The first edition is a fascinating historical document but a challenging read that demands wading through entries containing many words and phrases that are obscure, rare or now defunct.

A Grammar of the English Tongue.

By John Brightland. London, 1711.

One of the several English grammars of former centuries that I have found useful in understanding how our notions of grammar have evolved and how, occasionally, the rules laid out in those old grammars come back to haunt us today. The Cambridge University Library has a wonderful collection of old grammars, both originals and in facsimile form, and some are also available for consultation online in various different editions.

American National Corpus (http://www.anc.org/)

A huge database of contemporary American English texts searchable online. It has been very useful for comparisons between British and American English usage.

An Essay Towards a Practical English Grammar. Describing the Genius and Nature of the English tongue.

By James Greenwood, Sur-Master of St.-Paul's School. 1711.

Another useful historical source for checking what was considered good usage 250 years ago and how much still prevails today. Greenwood was quite prescriptive and prepared to label certain usages as bad grammar or *ungenteel and rude*.

A Short Introduction To English Grammar: With Critical Notes.

By the Right Rev. Robert Lowth D. D., Lord Bishop of Oxford. London, 1762.

This was a greatly influential English grammar which serves as an invaluable resource for anyone interested in how approaches to the description of English have varied over the centuries, as well as providing evidence for the study of the evolution of the grammar.

British National Corpus
(http://www.natcorp.ox.ac.uk/)

A 100-million-word demographically representative database of contemporary written and spoken English that has served me well over the years and is searchable online.

Cambridge Grammar of English: A Comprehensive Guide to Spoken and Written English Grammar and Usage.
By R. A. Carter and M. J. McCarthy. 2006. Cambridge: Cambridge University Press.

My colleague Ronald Carter and I spent seven years writing this and my head is still crammed with it. It has quite naturally informed, largely unconsciously, many of the statements made in this book. It got us into hot water with the purists when it was published and we had to defend our approach in the media. I cite it here as a tribute to Ron Carter rather than as an act of self-publicity.

Collins English Dictionary Online.
(https://www.collinsdictionary.com/dictionary/english/)

This is an excellent, up-to-date, freely searchable dictionary from a publisher that was a pioneer in the 1980s in the use of computerised corpora in dictionary production. The Collins-COBUILD dictionary for English language learners, published in 1987, broke new ground. The dictionary project was led by my great mentor, Professor John Sinclair (1933-2007), from whom I learnt my trade as language researcher and corpus analyst.

Elements of Rhetoric. By Richard Whately (1828).

The 1861 edition was used for the purposes of this book, published by the Southern Methodist Publishing House, Nashville, Tennessee.

This work is a reminder of the once very close relationship between rhetoric (the art of using language with the goal of persuasion via speaking or writing), grammar and style, an overlap that is often forgotten in modern-day applied linguistics but which survives in the American tradition of college composition classes and in the fields of literary stylistics and journalistic studies.

English Grammar, Adapted to the Different Classes of Learners.
By Lindley Murray. 1795. 16th Edition New York, 1809.

This background reading section lists a number of grammars from previous centuries because I firmly believe that we do ourselves no good service by thinking our present-day grammars are all we should consult. Murray's grammar was hugely popular and influential, and seeing what has changed since his day and that of our other grammarian ancestors is an important lesson in how language evolves and a warning that we should hesitate before disparaging recent and current trends.

English in Speech and Writing.
By Rebecca Hughes. London: Routledge. 1996.

A book that shows clearly how the grammar of speech, even in fairly formal situations such as Parliament, differs from the grammar written down. I have found it immensely useful over the years and its wealth of examples come to mind every time a pompous politician decries the current state of English grammar.

Google Books Ngram Viewer
(https://books.google.com/ngrams)

A great resource that lets you track the use of words across the centuries. See how words compete with one another, how they compare in frequency of use, how they come and go, how variants and different spellings evolve, all in a pleasant, easy-to-read visual display.

Hermes, Or, A Philosophical Inquiry Concerning Universal Grammar.
By James Harris. London, 1751.

Another of the old grammars that has provided fascinating insights into attitudes to grammar and ways of describing it. This one is jam-packed with quotations from Ancient Greek and Latin.

Oxford English Dictionary Second Edition on CD-ROM
(v. 4.0). Oxford University Press 2009.

Undoubtedly the most important resource for anyone researching the origins, evolution and usage of the vast treasure-house of English words and phrases. This is the version I have used. It is so easy to search.

Pamphlet for Grammar.
By William Bullokar. Imprinted at London: By Edmund Bollifant, 1586.

Held to be the first proper English grammar, this is an interesting if challenging read. Amongst other things, what it shows us is that the eight basic parts of speech that we are familiar with today were already established more than 400 years ago. Everything is described in terms of Latin (cases, declensions, etc.). It is available through the Oxford Text Archive. (http://ota.ox.ac.uk/desc/0025)

The English Grammar.
By Ben Jonson. 1640 (originally written in 1623 but published posthumously).

A window into grammatical description and attitudes all those centuries ago and another reminder that some of the issues that are still debated today are as old as the hills. For instance, Jonson championed speech over writing, stating, *Grammar is the art of true, and well speaking a language: the writing is but an accident*. Jonson's grammar is accessible via the excellent Scolar Press (Menston) edition of 1972 (quoted here, p.35).

The Royal English grammar: Containing what is necessary to the Knowledge of the English Tongue.
By James Greenwood, Sur-Master of St.-Paul's School. London, 1737.

Grammar manuals blossomed in the 18th century and, although generally prescriptive and founded on the notion that English should be squeezed into a Latin straitjacket, they contain invaluable insights into contemporary usage and attitudes and offer the potential for fruitful comparisons with grammar of the present day.

Shakespeare's Non-Standard English.
By Norman Blake. London: Continuum, 2004. Third edition 2006.

A wonderful dictionary of Shakespeare's use of informal and non-standard language, with detailed references to the original works and useful commentaries on forms and functions. The book reminds us that Shakespeare's grammar and vocabulary were not always high-flown and solemn but rich across the vast spectrum of English. It serves as an invaluable source of information on contemporary usage as well as Shakespeare's creativity with words and structures.

Printed in Great Britain
by Amazon